EXTRAORDINARY HOPE

EXTRAORDINARY

Hope

30 DAYS
*to Being
Strengthened
& Inspired*

Elizabeth Ann
WALLACE

NASHVILLE

NEW YORK · LONDON · MELBOURNE · VANCOUVER

EXTRAORDINARY HOPE

30 Days to Being Strengthened and Inspired

Published in New York, New York, by Morgan James Publishing. Morgan James is a trademark of Morgan James, LLC. www.MorganJamesPublishing.com

The Morgan James Speakers Group can bring authors to your live event. For more information or to book an event visit The Morgan James Speakers Group at www.TheMorganJamesSpeakersGroup.com.

ISBN 9781683509417 paperback
ISBN 9781683509424 eBook
Library of Congress Control Number: 2018930953

Cover Design by:
Chris Treccani
www.3dogcreative.net

Author photo by:
JeffreyGroundsPhotography.com

Interior Design by:
Christopher Kirk
www.GFSstudio.com

Professionally edited by:
Linda Gilden

In an effort to support local communities, raise awareness and funds, Morgan James
Publishing donates a percentage of all book sales for the life of each book to
Habitat for Humanity Peninsula and Greater Williamsburg.

Get involved today! Visit
www.MorganJamesBuilds.com

Disclaimer

Every reasonable effort has been made to determine copyright holders of excerpted materials and to secure permissions as needed. If any copyrighted materials have been inadvertently used in this work without proper credit given in one form or another, please notify Grace Anointed Ministries, LLC, in writing so that future printings of this work may be corrected accordingly.

Endorsements

"How would my life be different if I focused on hope? It's a powerful question posed by author Elizabeth Ann Wallace. And that question has led to a powerful book. In this 30-day devotional, the reader's focus is redirected and her soul is fed. This is the book we all need when life presses in and hope is obscured by situations. Definitely a book I'll return to again and again!"

EDIE MELSON,
AWARD-WINNING AUTHOR AND DIRECTOR
OF THE BLUE RIDGE MOUNTAINS CHRISTIAN WRITERS CONFERENCE

"I am a big fan of devotional books and have read many, but I cannot recall reading one like this before. Elizabeth Ann Wallace's *Extraordinary Hope* takes readers into great depth of thought, particularly with her in-depth references to the likes of C.S. Lewis, George Müller, and Tim Keller. Her devotions are genuinely thought provoking, and through this she is able to lead readers to a place of encouragement. She achieves her goal and genuinely points the way to hope. This is a great read!"

CHARLES N. WESTBROOK, D. MIN. AUTHOR,
PASTOR, SALUDA RIVER BAPTIST CHURCH, WEST COLUMBIA, SC
INTERNATIONAL MISSIONARY FOR 25 YEARS IN ASIA
17 YEARS PASTORING IN THE US
GRAD. CHARLESTON SOUTHERN UNIVERSITY, NEW ORLEANS BAPTIST THEOLOGICAL
SEMINARY, COLUMBIA INTERNATIONAL UNIVERSITY

"Devotions that make you really think seem far and few these days. Elizabeth Ann Wallace digs into the Word and makes it personal and thought provoking."

CINDY K. SPROLES
AWARD-WINNING AUTHOR AND SPEAKER
ACQUISITIONS EDITOR LIGHTHOUSE PUBLISHING OF THE CAROLINAS
ASHEVILLE CHRISTIAN WRITERS CONFERENCE

"In this 30 day devotional, Elizabeth Ann Wallace taps into a dynamic combination. Her use of scripture, as well as her practical writing style, will encourage and inspire. Ann is a powerful woman of God who shares in a way we can all relate to."

SHERRY POUNDSTONE
SPEAKER AND AUTHOR
CO-DIRECTOR OF CHRISTIAN COMMUNICATORS CONFERENCE

"What a wonderful book! It was a real blessing for me to read it."

CAROLINA NUNEZ GONZALEZ
MINISTERIO ROCA DEL PEDERNAL, SAN JOSE, COSTA RICA

"I just read daily devotions from Elizabeth Ann Wallace's *Extraordinary Hope* Devotional. Ann writes with such authority, boldness, and clarity that are derived truly from her own personal walk with Christ. Her insights on how to live close to God are penned to woo the most infant, or mature child of God, by providing each reader a specific biblical passage along with a guided way to meditate in prayer. You will grow from reading *Extraordinary Hope* Devotional!"

TERESA REDFEARN
LICENSED PSYCHO-EDUCATIONAL SPECIALIST
CERTIFIED CHILD AND ADOLESCENT TRAUMA PROFESSIONAL
NATIONALLY CERTIFIED SCHOOL PSYCHOLOGIST

"As I've read these devotional writings, I am strongly impressed that this is a God ordained, God-timed project. The richness of each daily devotional is more than a thought for the day. Through these inspired pages is the message of hope through stories, rich quotes, scriptures and the knitting together of all of it by the author as a conductor who conducts a beautiful symphony. The world needs to hear the message of hope found in the one and only true source. This is an act of spiritual warfare!"

REV. STEPHEN MORRISON
CO-FOUNDER AND EXEC DIRECTOR
HEALING FOR THE NATIONS

"Elizabeth Ann Wallace has written an encouraging book that stems from her spiritual journey that is sure to bring hope to a world that desperately needs hope. She clearly points to "our Lord Jesus Christ himself, and God our Father, who loved us and gave us eternal comfort and good hope through grace, comfort your hearts and establish them in every good work and word." (2 Thess. 2:16-17 ESV)."

DR. CHARLES BOSWELL
DIRECTOR OF PASTORAL CARE AND CHURCH HEALTH
COLORADO BAPTIST GENERAL CONVENTION

Foreword

━━━

❝I have the delight of writing the foreword for Ann's book, *Extraordinary Hope*. Hope is exactly what this world needs and yet, we seem so deprived of it. Religion has taught us to be afraid of getting our hopes up because if it doesn't come to pass, we will be disappointed. But the Bible teaches us that hope never disappoints! Getting our Hope level up is actually what we need! Having read this book, I felt a fresh hope rising in my own heart. Ann has done a wonderful job preparing to take you on a 30-day journey into Hope. Get ready, though, because this book is more than simply a 30-day journey into Hope; it's the launching pad into a lifetime of being Hope-filled. I once heard a quote that said, "The person with the most hope has the most influence". If you want to have influence and see your world changed around you, then I would encourage you to feast on the incredible substance that this book offers and allow Hope to saturate every part of your mind, soul, and spirit.

I have had the joy of meeting Ann several times over the past few years and when somebody lives what he or she writes; I am one to listen. Ann lives her life filled with what she writes. Just meeting her you feel Hope flowing from her life and your own hope tank gets filled to overflowing!

Thank you Ann for writing this book! I know it will enable so many people to become people, not just filled with Hope, but Hope-givers and influencers to this world."

Chris Gore

DIRECTOR HEALING MINISTRIES, BETHEL CHURCH, REDDING, CA
AUTHOR OF *WALKING IN SUPERNATURAL HEALING POWER AND OVERFLOW* A DAILY EXPERIENCE OF HEAVENS ABUNDANCE

Dedication

I dedicate this book to the beautiful Trinity:

My sweet Abba Father who loves me beyond words, Jesus, my Savior, the Word in flesh, who came and died that I might live and who is constantly interceding for me, and the sweet Holy Spirit, who lives in me and is my constant guide, teacher and comforter.

Without Them, this book would never have been written.

Introduction

Why is Hope so elusive? Why do we struggle to grasp it and hang on especially when we need it the most? Why does it seem to be only for the weak or faint at heart, those who have nothing else? But what if hope was more than just a feeling, what if it was something we could hang onto, count on, rely on, with everything in us. I'm not talking about something that's in our possession, that could ease our struggle or pain, but something beyond our grasp, outside of us that is so powerful, it gives us the strength to go on when our own strength is gone.

If we will focus on the reasons for our "hope" for the next 30 days and choose to live them, we will have begun to create a foundation of hope upon which to build. Hope for now and tomorrow. For whatever is to come, hope that will help us endure what we didn't even think was possible. Hope to give us strength in the midst of the storm.

"Hope" is the thing with feathers
By Emily Dickinson[1]

"Hope" is the thing with feathers -
That perches in the soul -
And sings the tune without the words -
And never stops - at all -

And sweetest - in the Gale - is heard -
And sore must be the storm -
That could abash the little Bird
That kept so many warm -

I've heard it in the chillest land -
And on the strangest Sea -
Yet - never - in Extremity,
It asked a crumb - of me.

DAY 1

"LORD, you know the hopes of the helpless. Surely
you will hear their cries and comfort them."
PSALM 10:17 NLT

Many in the world today do not know God. Some even think they do, by the words they have said, but their lifestyles indicate otherwise. In this chapter, the Psalmist talks about those who "through the pride of their countenance will not seek after God" and "God is not at all in his thoughts" (Psalm 10:4 KJV). Some are so self-focused they feel there is no need for a god in their life. They are not concerned with where they came from or the need for a Savior. The depth of their thinking never rises above their own needs, wants, or desires. Others feel the need to explain creation and how we got here; in terms they can wrap their minds around based on the scientific theories discovered thus far. Never thinking these theories might be incorrect or the truth of all creation may be beyond human capability to fully understand. Then there are those who hate the thought they might have to answer to a God who could be beyond them in His authority. Despising and discarding even the idea they have a Maker and Father who loves them beyond their comprehension. Yet His unconditional love is for even those who hate and reject Him. When they finally get to the point of despair and their ability to help themselves has fallen short is when they will cry out in the hope that someone might hear. God will listen, and He will comfort them.

C.S. Lewis struggled with the concept of God, and that struggle was evident in his earlier writings. On his belief as an atheist, he said, "If I can't trust my own thinking, of course I can't trust the arguments leading to atheism, and therefore have no reason to be an atheist, or anything else. Unless I believe in God, I cannot believe in thought: so I can never use thought to disbelieve in God."[2]

Lewis' religious pursuit was a rollercoaster of belief. From a religious family, Lewis was raised in the church, but at 15 he became an atheist, rebelling against Christianity as dutiful work. He was bitter, angry and resentful and did his best to prove God did not exist. But it was George MacDonald's book *Phantastes*, a work of fantasy literature, which helped Lewis begin to see there had to be some truth to God, for he could no longer believe everything was mere coincidence. From that point on Lewis started the turn from atheism and began to look again at religion. He didn't want to believe in God because so many things about God seemed illogical.

On the night he became a Christian, "Lewis vigorously resisted conversion, noting that he was brought into Christianity like a prodigal, 'kicking, struggling, resentful, and darting his eyes in every direction for a chance to escape.'"[3] He said, "I gave in, and admitted God was God, and knelt and prayed: perhaps, that night in 1929, the most dejected and reluctant convert in all England."[4]

Like most of us, our understanding about God and Christ doesn't come all at once, but slowly, over time our belief and understanding increase concerning spiritual truths. Knowing God is real meant other things about God had to be seriously considered, including Jesus Christ and Lewis' need for Him as his Savior. Then, on September 19, 1931, on an after-dinner walk with his friends, J. R. R. Tolkien (*The Lord of the Rings*) and Hugo Dyson, they discussed the truths about God and Christ hidden in legends and myths, until the wee hours of the morning. Tolkien believed these myths were from God and Lewis believed they were untrue. A few days later, Lewis wrote to an old friend and said he had "just passed from believing in God to definitely believing in Christ, in Christianity, and that his long talk with Dyson and Tolkien had a great deal to do with it."[5] From that moment on he became an ardent defender of the faith and Christian truth. His works today are some of the most beloved among Christian apologetics.

Our thoughts about God can be skeptical as well, disbelieving, angry or bitter. Many of us believed in God as children, wanting to go to heaven. We were scared and it seemed a simple thing to do, believe. But it can be a burden to bear, a weight to be carried, when we feel we have to earn our standing with God and our salvation because we want to be "good enough" to go to heaven. He knows we don't fully understand or yet fully believe, so He patiently places things and people in our lives to help lead us into revealing truths about Himself and His Son Jesus. His greatest desire is for us to know Him as our Father and enjoy the eternal relationship as His children.

Jesus says simply in Matthew 7:7, "Ask and it will be given to you; seek and you will find; knock and the door will be opened to you." When we seek Him, ask about Him and continue to knock on the doors that we want to see behind, our Father will lovingly answer and be found, sharing with us the answers we have been looking for and comfort us with hope that will never end.

DAY 2

"Blessed is the man who trusts in the LORD, and whose hope is the LORD. For he shall be like a tree planted by the waters, which spreads out its roots by the river, and will not fear when heat comes; but its leaf will be green, and will not be anxious in the year of drought, nor will cease from yielding fruit."
JEREMIAH 17:7-8 NKJV

According to Merriam's dictionary, "blessed" means, "enjoying happiness, bringing pleasure, contentment."[6] All of us would like that in our lives. So when we trust in Him and our hope is in Him, pleasure, happiness, and contentment are sure to come. Then the next verse goes on to describe what that blessed man looks like, a tree planted by the river, the source of its provision, not moved or changed negatively by anything that happens to it. Could we possibly be like this? Not moved or changed when difficulties come in our lives, without fear and anxiety, and never ceasing from yielding good (fruit) from our lives? Where do I sign up! Good, God!

Can this really be possible? It sounds too good to be true as the old adage goes. But have you tried it? Do you trust in the Lord and put your hope in Him? Or do you trust yourself to bring about all these things? And if so how is that working out for you?

George Müller, Director of the Ashley Downs Orphanage for Children in Bristol, England, and Christian Evangelist (1805-1898) says, "Either we trust in God, and in that case we neither trust in ourselves, nor in our fellow-men, nor in circumstances, nor in anything besides; or we do trust in one or more of these, and in that case do not trust in God."[7]

But George Müller did not always trust in God. As a young man, he was a liar, a thief, and a gambler, wanting nothing to do with religion or the Bible, even playing cards and drinking the night his mother died. George, at the age of 10, was stealing government money from his father who was a tax collector. He only went to church as was required, but Christianity meant nothing to him, having never heard the gospel, he didn't know he was to live by the Scriptures. George's father wanted him to have a lucrative position as a pastor in a church, so he sent him to divinity school. While at the school, George went to a private home prayer meeting that so moved him, an immediate transformation in his behavior occurred. He didn't know anything about God, but seeing someone pray on their knees at that meeting became the catalyst that brought him to his knees in confession as a sinner. Immediately, George stopped drinking, stealing, and lying and began his lifelong pursuit of following Christ. He hoped to become a missionary, but God had so much more in mind for him to do.

Müller preached in many churches, but never wanted a salary. He instead received unsolicited donations his entire life for all the work he did for the kingdom of God, living on only what would meet his needs. George started over 117 schools and distributed over a million New Testaments, Bibles, and religious tracts in his lifetime. George was meticulous in handling the things God gave him, keeping records of every donation given and how it was used in ministry. The children he cared for in the orphanages were well dressed, educated, and sent out when ready with a trunk, two changes of clothes, and a Bible. Many accused him of raising the poor above their station in society, and yet Jesus said to all of us in Matthew 19:21 ESV, "If you would be perfect, go, sell what you possess and give to the poor, and you will have treasure in heaven; and come, follow me."

George Müller lived his life taking care of the less fortunate and his theology was based strictly on the Bible. He opened his home to orphans until he could no longer contain all of them. Eventually, his housing expanded to include five orphanage houses, caring for over 2,050 children at any given time. Over the span of his lifetime, he cared for over 10,000 orphans. Everything he did he bathed in prayer, and whatever George asked, he knew God would answer.

Many times, he received unsolicited food donations only hours before they were needed to feed the children, further strengthening his faith in God. For example, on one well-documented occasion, they gave thanks for breakfast when all the children were sitting at the table, even though there was nothing to eat in the house. As they finished praying, the baker knocked on the door with sufficient fresh bread to feed everyone, and the milkman gave them plenty of fresh milk because his cart broke down in front of the orphanage.[8]

The last 17 years of his life, George left the orphanage care in the hands of his daughter while he traveled over 200,000 miles around the world as an evangelist.

Extraordinary faith leads to extraordinary acts of amazing kingdom building. We often think these brave mighty men of God were born that way, but so often they come from backgrounds just like many of us. God can use any one of us to change the world, all we have to do is trust Him for the outcome and exhibit faith in the face of whatever adversity comes our way. Trust in God, hope in Him and believe that no matter what happens, God's got you and will bring incredible fruitfulness from your life no matter what difficulties you face.

DAY 3

*"Happy is he who has the God of Jacob for his help,
whose hope is in the LORD his God."*
PSALM 39:7 JUBILEE BIBLE 2000

I don't know about you, but I can use all the help I can get. Not half-hearted help, but help that makes me happy. Not the kind people offer where they want credit for helping, don't really give 100 percent, quit on you in the middle of helping, or back out altogether. With the society becoming more and more self-focused, those who offer to help are usually looking for something in return. Fewer and fewer just help out of the kindness of their hearts. Knowing the Lord would be my help if my hope is in Him and that I would be happy, doesn't suggest half-heartedness. This would be the help I really need when I need it. Being happy can mean pleasure, contentment, fortunate, convenient, and timely. In the following story, the Lord's help was definitely fortunate and timely.

September 11, 2001, began like any other ordinary day for Stanley Praimnath, a Christian, who worked at a bank on the 81st floor of the South Tower of the World Trade Center. He got ready, said his prayers on the way to work, and headed up to his office. No sooner than he got there and began retrieving his messages, he looked out his office window to see fire falling through the North Tower that seemed to be coming from the roof. His boss worked in that building, so he called him to see what was going on. No answer. He decided it might be best if he exited the building just in case something was wrong, so he suggested to the temp working with him that they should proceed downstairs. When they got on the elevator, several other people felt something might be wrong and headed down the stairwell too. Once on the ground floor, the security guard assured all it was just an accident, and it was under control. He sent them back up to their offices. Once back in his office and on the phone, he looked out his window again. He saw a plane coming directly toward his building. It was so close he could see the markings on the wing. It appeared to be about 100 yards away and moving in slow motion when Stanley said, "Lord, you take control, I can't help myself here."[9] He then dove under his desk, curled up and waited for the impending disaster.

Miraculously, he was unhurt but was covered with a pile of rubble. He could see the wing of the plane on fire in his department and knew he needed to get out as soon as possible. Stanley continued to cry out for the Lord's help. He then received incredible strength to shake off all of the debris that covered him. His office looked like a war zone, and everything Stanley tried to walk over was collapsing.

He finally saw a light, which he at first thought might be his guardian angel, but turned out to be someone with a flashlight. Even if Stanley could get through all the debris, all the exits were blocked, and there was a wall between him and the light. He was finding it difficult to breathe now, as the fumes and smoke were affecting his oxygen levels.

On his knees, Stanley prayed again, "Lord, you've got to help me. You've brought me this far, help me get to the staircase."[10] He and the person with the flashlight then asked the Lord to give him the strength to break through the wall. He got up and felt incredible power come over him and he punched his way through. He was able to climb out the hole, but he and his new friend still had 81 flights of stairs to descend before they would be out of the building.

When they reached the ground floor, firefighters were telling everyone to run out of the building. The problem was, at this point, the concourse was on fire. So Stanley and his friend wet themselves under the building's sprinkler system and ran through the flames. They didn't stop running until they were two blocks away and their hands touched the gate at Trinity Church. For the first time, they turned around, and as soon as they did, they saw South Tower collapse.

> "For some divine reason, I know, beyond a shadow of a doubt, that the good Lord's mighty hand turned the plane a fraction from where I was standing," said Stanley. "Because when it crash-landed, it was just 20 feet from me. I don't care

who would rationalize—what people would say now or years from now, but I know it was the handiwork of the Lord that turned that plane. My Lord Jesus is bigger than the Trade Center and His finger can push a plane aside."[11]

Who is your help in time of need? Is it yourself or someone you may or may not be able to count on? The Lord has more at His disposal than we could ever imagine. Even though we try to plan our days, we never know how they will turn out. I can't think of a better solution than having a God I can count on to help me in my time of need and knowing nothing is impossible with Him.

DAY 4

"Let your hope keep you joyful, be patient in your troubles, and pray at all times."
ROMANS 12:12 GNT

How do you remain joyful in the midst of trouble, patiently get through it, and pray all the time? Most of us would be the opposite, grieving, feeling entitled to self-pity, and anxious about what to do next. We certainly wouldn't feel like praying about it, wondering, if prayer had worked in the first place, why did I even have to go through this? What we have learned in the world about how to respond is not what the Bible teaches. Instead, what the Bible teaches as the way to live is the complete opposite of what comes naturally. What does it look like to be joyful even in the midst of pain and or difficulty, praying, expecting God, your hope, to come through?

According to Tim Keller, author of *Walking with God through Pain and Suffering*,

"While other worldviews lead us to sit in the midst of life's joys, foreseeing the coming sorrows, Christianity empowers its people to sit in the midst of this world's sorrows, tasting the coming joy."[12]

> A great example of this came one Sunday morning in a small town. Massena, one of Napoleon's generals, suddenly appeared with eighteen thousand men before an Austrian town which had no means of defense. The town council had nearly decided to surrender when the old dean of the church reminded them that it was Easter and begged them to hold services as usual and to leave the trouble in God's hands. This they did; and the French hearing the church bells ringing joyfully concluded that an Austrian army had come to relieve the place and quickly broke camp. Before the bells ceased ringing, all the Frenchmen had vanished.[13]

Can you imagine the elation from their deliverance? The shouts of joy that must have erupted from the church-goers as they realized they had been saved by their Heavenly King! Putting their hope in their God to save them while they focused on worship on Easter Sunday morning, patiently trusting Him and praying. And yet, we do the same when we put our hope in God every time we look past our current trouble and instead worship Him, trusting Him to take care of all of the trouble concerning us. Our part in our life's dramas is to worship; His part is to provide for our needs, whether through deliverance or showing us the way in whatever concerns us.

Our joy comes from our hope in Jesus. Looking at Him and trusting Him to get us through is the only thing keeping us from drowning within ourselves. Hope preserves our sanity and keeps us healthy both emotionally and physically. We can't be anxious and caught up in the problem, making ourselves sick with worry.

"Be anxious for nothing, but in everything by prayer and supplication, with thanksgiving, let your requests be made known to God; and the peace of God, which surpasses all understanding, will guard your hearts and minds through Christ Jesus" (Philippians 4:6-7 NKJV).

Hope in Christ is the beginning of getting through the difficult times and showing others the way to get through theirs. Focusing on the hope, which is Jesus, keeps us joyful, helps us to be patient when times are tough and to pray or focus on God all the time.

DAY 5

"You are my hiding place and my shield;
I hope in Your word."
PSALM 119:114 NKJV

Many of us enjoyed hide and seek when we were children, but how many of us wish we could remain hidden at times? Maybe we lived in a home where hiding kept us from harm or abuse, and it was the only time we felt safe. Some of us are still trying to hide from whatever we fear could happen if we came out. We feel vulnerable and exposed around others. We are so afraid, it's hard to believe there is anything we can trust to protect us. God's Word says He will be our hiding place and shield if we put our hope in His Word. If we read it, believe it, and receive it as truth, He can act on our behalf. He can keep us covered and safe, defending us from our enemies by being a shield of defense. That's total protection, until we are ready or need to come out and can fight with His strength.

In the story of David, the future king of Israel, his enemy, King Saul, came into a cave in which David was hiding, to relieve himself, but never saw David. David then proceeds to cut off a piece of the King's robe, as proof that he could have killed him, but chose not to touch the Lord's anointed. Could that have been a test to see if David would indeed trust God for his future as Israel's king, even when it seemed as if God brought his enemy to Him?

Many of us know Corrie Ten Boom's story, *The Hiding Place*. Her Dutch Christian family hid hundreds of people during the time of the Holocaust. God used her family to provide a modern day place of hiding and a shield to those who were led to their home. Even though Corrie and her family were found to be hiding Jews and others involved in the resistance movement, those they had hidden were never exposed. Ten days after, Corrie, her sister Betsie and father were discovered by the Nazis, her father died. Corrie and Betsie were sent to a concentration camp in February 1944. After solitary confinement for Corrie for three months and having transferred to different concentration camps, she and her sister finally ended up at Ravensbruck, a women's labor camp. Corrie and Betsie held nightly worship services with a Bible they had somehow managed to bring into the camp.

> While at Ravensbruck, Betsie ten Boom began to discuss plans with her sister for after the war for a place of healing. Betsie's health continued to deteriorate and she died on December 16, 1944, at the age of 59.[14] Before she died, she told Corrie, "There is no pit so deep that He [God] is not deeper still." Fifteen days later on the first

> Corrie was released. Afterwards she was told that her release was due to a clerical error and that a week later, all the women in her age group were sent to the gas chambers.[15]

Corrie knew her God and trusted him even in the face of the loss of her family. She knew He was ultimately in charge of her life and whatever He decided she knew would be His best for her. In her life, she lived and saw the fulfillment of Psalm 32:7 "You are my hiding place; you will protect me from trouble and surround me with songs of deliverance."

God's shield of protection is the only thing that can stand in the face of your enemies. He will not let you down, when you trust Him as your shield.

"...take up the shield of faith with which you can extinguish all the flaming arrows of the evil one" (Ephesians 6:16 CSB).

He knows how much evil truly is out there. He wants to protect us, but knowing His Word is what gives us hope. He will be a hiding place and a shield for us, even when life doesn't turn out like we planned.

DAY 6

"But now, Lord, what do I look for?
My hope is in you."
PSALM 39:7

I'm sure most of us can say we have been at a crossroad in our lives where we weren't sure what to look for, where each of our choices could lead us in different directions. Not knowing our futures, we can become really concerned about which way to go. Some of us look to psychics or mediums and horoscopes. Some of us see everything as a sign of the direction we should take or the choice we should make. But what really should we look at to help us know the right way, the right choice? A choice or direction that won't come with bad consequences, heartbreak or financial disaster would be ideal. Does anybody really know our future?

God says in the Scriptures before we were born He knew us. He placed us in our mother's wombs with plans for our future. King David who wrote this psalm was calling out to God to make his life count. That he knew life here on earth was but a vapor on the eternal timeline, that so much of what we strive for and accumulate means nothing when we are gone. If nothing here holds lasting significance, what do I look for? King David came to the conclusion we can only put our hope in the Lord, who knows our future, what is best for us here and what we will do that will last for all of eternity. God will direct us where to look, what is best, and what we can count on. He knows how this will all turn out.

In a wonderful prayer, expressed by Thomas Merton in his book *Thoughts of Solitude*, he says,

> "My Lord God, I have no idea where I am going. I do not see the road ahead of me. I cannot know for certain where it will end. Nor do I really know myself, and the fact that I think that I am following your will does not mean that I am actually doing so. But I believe that the desire to please you does in fact please you. And I hope I have that desire in all that I am doing. I hope that I will never do anything apart from that desire. And I know that if I do this you will lead me by the right road, though I may know nothing about it. Therefore will I trust you always, though I may seem to be lost and in the shadow of death. I will not fear, for you are ever with me, and you will never leave me to face my perils alone."[16]

Even though some question Merton's journey of faith, it was clear He trusted God alone for His guidance. God in His unending grace gives us a wide berth of freedom in our quest for more of Him. With the Holy Spirit as our guide, He brings us back to the truth when we fall in errors of our understanding of Him. None of us have yet attained the perfection of Christ, but continuing to seek Him, knowing He alone is our hope keeps us on the right path to eternal life.

DAY 7

"By awesome deeds you answer us with righteous-
ness, O God of our salvation, the hope of all the
ends of the earth and of the farthest seas;"
PSALM 65:5 ESV

The God who saves us and is the hope of all on earth, answers us with awesome, morally right, and justifiable deeds. Many stories are in the Bible of amazing things God has done, from the truly miraculous to the simple, yet profound. He longs to show us great and mighty things, but so often we live in disbelief that He will or that He can. We know the stories in the Bible, but either we don't believe them, look at them as allegories, or believe they only happened during that time. God says in His Word He is the same, yesterday, today and tomorrow. He is not limited by time and therefore does not lock what can happen into a season of time. The sooner we learn that, the more our faith will increase.

We live in an environment focused on the negative rather than the positive. This has also translated over to our perception of God and what He didn't do rather than what He did. Instead of rejoicing over the good that comes from a tragedy, we focus on all that was lost. In the face of natural disasters there is always great sadness and mourning, but we gain such hope in seeing those who survive.

In reading over many stories, it is interesting to me how many involve the hand of God. I'll never forget December 26, 2004, when a tsunami hit Thailand, several other countries and islands. Almost 300,000 people were killed that day. The survivor stories have been amazing testimonies of God's intervention on behalf of those who sought Him as the source of their hope.

One such instance occurred with Jordan Bilyeu, 17, just sitting on the beach reading a book when he noticed suddenly the ocean wasn't there. The next thing he saw was an enormous wall of water coming toward him on the beach. Before he knew it, he was taken over by the gigantic wave and hit with all types of debris while he was underwater. He prayed for God to help him and not let him die. Just as he thought it was over, his head popped out of the water and he could see a palm tree. He grabbed the tip of a branch and prayed again that God would give him the strength to hold on. When he realized the water was continuing to go inland, he got on the palm tree and rode it in toward the land. Upon coming close to a hotel, a lady inside reached out of a window and pulled him in. One of his fingertips had been severed, which he doused with vodka from a mini fridge and covered with a sock, because he was anxious to go out and rescue others.

Within two hours Jordan and several others had helped 13 people get to safety.

Of the 200 people on the beach that day, Jordan was one of only two to survive. "I'm thankful to be alive," Jordan says. "But I'm even more thankful that God used me to help others. God changed my life. I owe my life to him and I'll go wherever he wants me to go—even into the face of another storm."[17]

In light of all Jordan went through, it is interesting to note that he would do it again. When we KNOW God is our salvation, our hope, and can do amazing, awesome deeds to answer us or rescue us, our focus is no longer on ourselves, but on our God and whatever He has for us.

DAY 8

*"May the God of hope fill you with all joy and peace
in believing, so that by the power of the Holy Spirit
you may abound in hope."*
ROMANS 15:13 ESV

Skepticism is more the norm than the exception today.
With increased access to the media and information
about current events, people find it more complicated to
locate trustworthy sources giving us any hope, much less
joy and peace. In fact, many sources we thought to be
unbiased in their presentation of corroborated information
have been exposed as fraudulent or only representing their
opinions. What is so concerning about this is, the more we
tune out what is out there, the more we will be uninformed
about what we truly may need to know. And in the moment
when we need something to stand on, we won't know what
we actually believe. So where do we turn? What can we
believe is really truth? How do we turn our fear, dread, and
uncertainty into joy, peace, and hope?

Past history is a measurement upon which the truth can
be sifted, what has stood the test of time and proven itself

both in man and nature to be constant. We cannot look to ourselves for the strength we need to endure tribulation and trials, but only upon that which is greater than ourselves. We are made to find our Maker and in Him, He will supply the power to believe and give us hope no matter what we must face. True believers who have faced enduring hardships as well as everyday trials will attest to supernatural power and endurance that produces joy and peace in the midst of incredible circumstances.

Richard Wurmbrand, the founder of Voice of the Martyrs, which aids Christians around the world who are persecuted for their faith, wrote first-hand as a persecuted believer just how important belief in God was in his book *Tortured for Christ*. Arrested by Secret Police of the communist regime, which had taken over Romania, he was placed in solitary confinement for three years with no light, windows, or sound, 12 feet underground. The guards even wore felt on the bottom of their shoes so that not a sound could be heard. He said he kept himself sane by exercising his mind and soul and creating a sermon every day and delivering it every night. He was then moved to a small communal cell with over 200 other prisoners in the most wretched conditions imaginable for the next 5 ½ years.

> During his imprisonment, he was beaten and tortured. Psychological torture included incessant broadcasting of phrases denouncing Christianity and praising Communism. His body bore the scars of physical torture for the rest of his life. For example, he later recounted having the

soles of his feet beaten until the flesh was torn off, then the next day beaten again to the bone. This prolific writer said there were not words to describe that pain.[18]

After being imprisoned one other time, Richard was finally granted amnesty and eventually testified in Washington, D.C., before a U.S. Senate subcommittee about persecution of Christians in communist countries. He devoted the rest of his life to becoming a voice for the persecuted church.

At the end of any means to help themselves, you would think if there was anything other than Jesus Christ as their hope to help them find peace and joy, we would have heard about it by now. Yes, some have sacrificed themselves for other faiths and even been persecuted, but those that have been brutally martyred and persecuted for the Christian faith have attested that there was a supernatural power that enabled their spirits to be sustained in unaccountable joy, peace, and hope. Hope that they never wavered from and that convinced so many others of the truth of their beliefs.

DAY 9

*"Be strong and of good courage,
and He shall strengthen your heart,
all you who hope in the LORD."*
PSALM 31:24 NKJV

When I looked at this verse, the Holy Spirit brought to mind the story of Todd Beamer in the book *Let's Roll,* written by his wife Lisa Beamer. In the midst of our nation's greatest terrorist attack, one plane never reached its terrorist-intended destination due to the courage of its passengers. If it had been you or me, would we have had the courage to do what they did in light of our imminent deaths?

This last verse of the 31st Psalm shared how David felt surrounded by the enemy, but it could have just as easily been written about that day on Flight 93. It is amazing when you see the eternal Word of God applied to a modern day situation, inserting your name, and knowing God was aware long before this day how much you would need to know He already knew what was coming. Lord, there is none like You! No other god can make the claims you do and be there for your people. No other god is omnipotent, omniscient, and omnipresent.

Todd Beamer, raised in a Christian home, headed out on a business trip September 11, 2001, and was planning on being home that night. He could have left the night before, but opted to spend the time with his family, pregnant wife Lisa, and his two sons. Todd's flight, United Flight 93, was delayed by 42 minutes due to runway traffic. Six minutes after takeoff, while his plane was climbing to cruising altitude, another plane was crashing into the North Tower of the World Trade Center. Fifteen minutes after the North Tower of the WTC was hit, a second plane was flown into the South Tower. The pilot of United Flight 93 received an alert to beware of cockpit intrusion and what was going on with other airplanes, when the terrorists burst through, killing both the pilot and copilot. The terrorists then moved all of the passengers to the back of the plane and told them not to try anything because they had a bomb. Within six minutes the plane had changed course and was now headed to Washington, D.C., instead of California.

Passengers on the plane made phone calls to loved ones, who in turn informed them about what was going on at the World Trade Center and the Pentagon. Beamer, tried to make a call on a back of the seat plane phone, only to be connected to an air phone operator. He then informed her of what was happening on their plane. When the plane veered sharply, Beamer panicked and thought they were going down. Following this, he and the other passengers and flight crew decided to act. Not sure whether the White

House or Capitol may be in jeopardy, they decided to storm the hijackers and take over control of the plane.

> "'…I don't think we are going to get out of this thing,' Todd said. 'I'm going to have to go out on faith.'"[19]

He proceeded to tell the phone operator, they planned to jump the guy with the bomb. He then asked the operator to recite the Lord's Prayer with him and followed with reciting the 23rd Psalm prompting others to join in. He then said the infamous line now quoted by so many, "Let's roll!" From voice recordings we know they stormed the cockpit and shortly the plane crashed into an open field at 580 miles an hour killing everyone onboard. It was only 15-20 minutes flying time away from Washington, D.C. and what could have been another national disaster.

When we know the God we serve and rely totally on Him for our strength and reserve in times of crisis, He always comes through. We may not have the outcome we were expecting or hoping for, but the hope it brings to so many because of our faith is well worth the cost.

DAY 10

*"For in You, O LORD, I hope; You will hear, O Lord
my God."*
PSALM 38:15 NKJV

To be deaf and blind is a tragedy to which most of us
can't relate. We rely on our senses for so much understanding and delight in what we experience. To be without
one would be bad enough, but two is more than most of us
can fathom. Helen Keller came to mind when I first saw
this verse. Not knowing why, until I looked in my Bible and
saw the previous verses where David describes his plight
as the light gone from his eyes and he is like a deaf man
and cannot speak nor hear. David then prays this verse to
the Lord as his only hope, knowing the Lord will listen and
will answer him. The Lord's answer may not come in the
package we expected, but He will answer.

Helen Keller was born in 1880, but at 19 months old she
contracted an acute illness, thought to have possibly been
scarlet fever or meningitis. It left her both blind and deaf.
In 1886, Keller's mother read an account of a successful

education of a blind and deaf woman and sent her daughter, Helen and her father to an ear, nose and throat specialist in Baltimore. He then referred them to Alexander Graham Bell who had been working with deaf children. Bell then directed them to Perkins School for the Blind where they found Anne Sullivan, who herself was visually impaired, to become Helen's instructor.

Anne arrived at Helen's house in 1887 and began teaching her how to communicate by spelling the name of the object in one hand while Helen would hold the object in the other hand. After many frustrating attempts to understand what Anne was teaching her, Helen finally understood the connection. It was just the beginning of a lifelong pursuit of education and excelling in communication. She went to several schools and was the first blind and deaf student ever to graduate with a Bachelor of Arts degree. Helen learned to speak and was a world famous speaker and author. She was an advocate for the deaf and those with disabilities as well as many other causes and founder for several associations, including the American Civil Liberties Union.

Keller proved to the world that deaf people could all learn to communicate, that they were capable of doing things that hearing people could do, and that they could survive in a hearing world. One of the most famous deaf people in history, she has long been a role model for the deaf, giving so many hope.

A favorite story about Helen Keller concerns her first introduction to the gospel. When Helen, who was both blind and deaf, learned to communicate, Anne Sullivan, her teacher, decided it was time for her to hear about Jesus Christ. Anne called for Phillips Brooks, the most famous preacher in Boston. With Sullivan interpreting for him, he talked to Helen Keller about Christ. It wasn't long until a smile lit up her face. Through her teacher she said, "Mr. Brooks, I have always known about God, but until now I didn't know His name."[20]

The Lord had already been communicating with Helen before she even knew His name and even before she knew how to communicate with Him. We limit God by what we think He can do based on our perceptions of how we communicate. We think He communicates like us and will convey His answers in the way of our own understanding. Never once can we see the whole picture. We cannot fathom how many will be effected by God hearing the longing of our hearts and answering us in the way that will bring us the most joy.

In one of Helen's lectures, she spoke of the joy life gave her. How thankful she was for what she had and the joy of service and happiness it gave her to help and do for others. Truly, God knew what would bring Helen great joy and fulfillment. He heard her cry to communicate and fulfilled it beyond her expectations.

DAY 11

"Behold, the eye of the LORD is on those who fear
him, on those who hope in his steadfast love,"
PSALM 33:18 ESV

Most of the time when I picture the Lord, I picture Him on the throne, delegating to others for His work to be done. He is so busy, it's hard enough to comprehend that He hears all of my prayers, much less has His eye on me as well as everyone else who reveres Him and puts their hope in His unwavering love for them. In the previous verses before these two, the Bible says, "From heaven the LORD looks down and sees all mankind; from his dwelling place he watches all who live on earth—he who forms the hearts of all, who considers everything they do" (Psalm 33:13-15).

Not only is His eye on those who hope in Him, He is watching all His creation in order that He may work all things out for our good, to those who love God and are called according to His purpose (Romans 8:28). I think our picture of the Lord is much harsher than He really is. He adores and loves all of His creation. This verse reminds me of the gospel song "His Eye is on the Sparrow." The theme of the song is inspired by the words of David in the Psalms and Jesus in the Gospel of Matthew in the Bible:

> I will instruct thee and teach thee in the way which thou shalt go: I will guide thee with mine eye (Psalm 32:8 KJV).

> Look at the birds of the air; they neither sow nor reap nor gather into barns, and yet your heavenly Father feeds them. Are you not of more value than they (Matthew 6:26 ESV)?

> Are not two sparrows sold for a farthing? and one of them shall not fall on the ground without your Father. But the very hairs of your head are all numbered. Fear ye not therefore, ye are of more value than many sparrows (Matthew 10:29–31 KJV).

Civilla Martin, who wrote the lyrics, said about her inspiration to write the song based on the scriptures:

> Early in the spring of 1905, my husband and I were sojourning in Elmira, New York. We contracted a deep friendship for a couple by the name of Mr. and Mrs. Doolittle—true saints of God. Mrs. Doolittle had been bedridden for nigh twenty years. Her husband was an incurable cripple who had to propel himself to and from his business in a wheelchair. Despite their afflictions, they lived happy Christian lives, bringing inspira-

tion and comfort to all who knew them. One day while we were visiting with the Doolittles, my husband commented on their bright hopefulness and asked them for the secret of it. Mrs. Doolittle's reply was simple: "His eye is on the sparrow, and I know He watches me." The beauty of this simple expression of boundless faith gripped the hearts and fired the imagination of Dr. Martin and me. The hymn "His Eye Is on the Sparrow" was the outcome of that experience.[21]

This song written in 1905 was honored in the Grammy Hall of Fame in 2010. Most notably sung by Mahalia Jackson and Ethel Waters it was the last original recording by Whitney Houston four months before her death in 2012.

I believe some songs are a direct download from heaven. Our spirits will often sing to comfort us in what we do not understand in our flesh. Millions of people have found comfort from knowing the Lord watches over them through this song. It has brought the reality of His love to whatever they may be going through, whether it be times of suffering or discouragement, pain, or loneliness. We can rest assured that He, who is our hope, is lovingly keeping an eye on us.

DAY 12

"We wait in hope for the LORD;
He is our help and our shield."
PSALM 33:20

Waiting is not a strength for most of us. It requires patience and, in today's world where speed is king, no one has time to wait. In fact, it's a value that has been quickly lost in our society where so many things can be instantly attained. But as this verse says, when we wait in hope for the Lord, He will be our help and a shield for us. Shields are not something most of us think about except militarily. A shield can be something visible or invisible. For example, scientists have found an invisible, protective shield 7200 miles above earth that cloaks it, protecting it from damaging superfast "killer" electrons that could harm astronauts, or fry our satellites.

> "'It's almost like these electrons are running into a glass wall in space,' lead author Professor Daniel Baker said in a news release. 'Somewhat like the shields created by force fields on Star Trek that

were used to repel alien weapons, we are seeing an invisible shield blocking these electrons. It's an extremely puzzling phenomenon.'"[22]

Even after several theories were proposed, scientists still have not discovered what is providing this protective shield. So many times, we have no idea what God shielded us from to keep us from harm. Countless documented stories of those in the military tell how God provided a shield of protection for them from the enemy.

One Major in the US Army said,

"During my recent year of deployment to Afghanistan, I experienced His Divine protection on a number of occasions." "When chased by three Afghani personnel while alone, I prayed an excerpt from Psalm 91, and immediately three Marines came running toward me, causing my potential assailants to flee. The next day I learned there were no Marines in the area." "I survived a rocket attack, seeing the rocket land less than 100m away from me without a single scratch. I commanded one of the most mobile units in Afghanistan, running hundreds of missions via air and convoy for an entire year without a single casualty, causing the Headquarters and all of its subordinate units to earn safety awards. In a final act of protection, my unit unexpectedly left Afghanistan a few days early. We left in the morning, and that evening, during the time our unit usually dined together, the dining facility tent was hit with a rocket."[23]

Psalm 91 is a psalm of protection and is often quoted by military and first responders in the line of duty. Testimony after testimony has been attributed to the protection many have felt after reciting this psalm including lives being miraculously saved. In *13 Hours; The Secret Soldiers of Benghazi*, the real life story of what happened in Benghazi, Libya, at the US Diplomatic Compound and the CIA Annex is portrayed. It relays the courage it took to stand and fight for their lives and the lives of others endangered by the takeover of Islamic extremists. "Tanto" and "Oz," two survivors of the ordeal, said their faith in God got them through. They said they both felt God's angels around them t protecting them. Mortars, one of which fell within 15 feet of "Oz", bombarded the CIA Annex. Normally this would kill everything within 21 feet, yet he walked out alive. Grievously wounded, "Oz says that '[God's] presence was there with me. It was what got me through.'"[24]

Soldiers and others, who visited the sites of the attacks and where the survivors were holding out, could not believe they were still alive. Bullet holes covered every inch of where they had been.

When we wait and hope for the Lord, He truly can protect us in unimaginable ways. Ways that don't make logical sense and could not be proven scientifically, truly beyond our comprehension to understand even with today's best minds. Waiting in hope is belief that the Lord will come through, we don't know how and we don't need to know when, we just know that He will be our help and our shield.

DAY 13

"but the LORD takes pleasure in those who fear
him, in those who hope in his steadfast love."
PSALM 147:11 ESV

In some Bible translations it says the Lord delights, favors, values, or is pleased with those who fear (revere) Him. In the previous verse, 10, it says, "His pleasure is not in the strength of the horse, nor his delight in the legs of a man." This verse is probably referring to cavalry and infantry, the strength of a man's army according to one commentary. God is interested more in the character of a man rather than his capacity.

In fact, this verse is in the middle of a chapter expounding on some of the great things God does such as determining "the number of stars" and calling "each of them by name." He "heals the brokenhearted and binds up their wounds." God is "mighty in power, and His understanding has no limit. The Lord sustains the humble and casts the wicked to the ground." "He covers the sky with clouds," supplies the rain and "makes grass grow on hills." God "provides food for the cattle and for the young ravens when they call." "He sends His command to the earth" and "His word runs swiftly." The Good Lord spreads snow and scatters frost, hurls hail, stirs up breezes, and makes waters to flow. And this is the short list. So many things we take for granted or somehow don't attribute to be in God's control. The psalmist, David, here is reminding us of why we should revere the Lord our God for all the great things He has done.

Some of us have trouble with those in authority and don't believe we need anyone in authority over us. But recognizing that someone, such as God, is in authority and is governing or watching over things for our good, can be relieving. Instead of the pressure being on us to make everything happen, all we have to do is be thankful we have someone who loves us so much. He wants to do those things and delights in us when we recognize Him and put our hope in His constant love for us. I mean really, could we possibly do any of those things stated in the Psalm? It truly is amazing that a God so big, who has supplied so much, would be just delighted in us knowing Him.

I can hear some of you now, "Is His ego so big that we need to praise Him? I mean come on what kind of narcissist God is that?"

Our recognizing who He is and that He is worthy of our praise is not because He needs it, it is because He knows it's what we were created for and brings us into relationship with Him. He knows when we truly know who He is, in our worship of Him; we will not be focused on self, but on Him. Our focus on worship then allows Him to fill us with

His goodness and love, bringing us into great peace and rest and the fullness of the plans He has for us.

Here are a few quotes from those who fear the Lord:

"The remarkable thing about God is that when you fear God, you fear nothing else, whereas if you do not fear God, you fear everything else." –Oswald Chambers[25]

"Fear God and your enemies will fear you." –Benjamin Franklin

"I believe in God. I don't fear man, I fear God." –Denzel Washington[26]

"We cannot grasp the true meaning of the divine holiness by thinking of someone or something very pure and then raising the concept to the highest degree we are capable of. God's holiness is not simply the best we know infinitely bettered. We know nothing like the divine holiness. It stands apart, unique, unapproachable, incomprehensible, and unattainable. The natural man is blind to it. He may fear God's power and admire His wisdom, but His holiness he cannot even imagine." –A. W. Tozer[27]

"Fear God, and where you go men shall think they walk in hallowed cathedrals." –Ralph Waldo Emerson[28]

The more we know of God, the more we love Him. It can take a while for the fog of what seems to be truth about which the world says He is to clear before you come into the revelation of who He really is. Like the delight we experience when our children love us and recognize the things we do for them because we love them, He delights knowing we revere Him and know He is steadfast in His love toward us. And it is in that great love we know we can place our hope that moves us to fear and be in awe of Him.

DAY 14

"The hope of the righteous shall be *gladness: but
the expectation of the wicked shall perish."*
PROVERBS 10:28 KJV

This verse speaks to me of what is to come for both the
righteous, who are good, morally right, virtuous and the
wicked, who are evil, morally wrong, and corrupt. I've never
met anyone who lived a good, moral life who wasn't glad in
the end for the hope for which he lived. I have, however, met
many a person who chose his or her own way, refusing to
live according to God's ways. In the end, they had nothing
to place hope in except for possessions and relationships,
which, of course, he or she couldn't take with them when
they died. Granted a person may have accumulated material
wealth and even did some good deeds, but there was no real
lasting happiness in it. Their hope was within themselves
to provide and fulfill all their needs, yet the sacrifices they
made in their lives proved in the end not to be worth the
gain. Why is that? Why can't we do some good and have
some things and be happy? Of course, we are happy for the

moment, but it doesn't last, because shortly thereafter we are looking for the next thing to make us happy.

I remember, personally being so angry with God that the only way was His way. Following His rules and doing it His way wasn't fun and I was bored. Heaven or hell, what kind of choice was that? Not realizing at the time, I didn't really know Him and the life He offered. Trust me, you are either living for the Lord or you are living for the enemy, Satan. You may think you are making your own choices, but you feel bound, angry, and resentful. The highs are short and the lows are long. It's amazing how long you can live like this just trying to prove to yourself you don't need God for your happiness.

But don't take my word for it. How many of us have heard of those near death experiences (NDE), where people died while being operated on or were dead for a few minutes, but then came back? The Bible speaks many times about people who rose from the dead. In fact, on the day of Jesus' resurrection, many rose out of their graves to testify of Him. No doubt, people who speak of the afterlife are witnesses of life after physical death. In case after case, many tell of unconditional love, peace, a sense of rest, bright light and awareness of their death and they can see what is happening to their body. For others, they experience a place of incredible darkness, where there is horrible screaming, intense heat, and smoke with people burning in fire, but not being consumed. Interestingly, the people who experienced the darkness of hell, either had no spiritual life or were in sin living apart from the truth of God's Word. Even some who doubted the validity of those who claimed to have these experiences have ironically gone through the experience themselves. In fact, since ancient times, 95% of world cultures have recorded some mention of NDEs. Isn't it interesting these testimonies confirm the hope of the righteous is gladness. We have much to look forward to both now and in the afterlife, when our physical bodies are dead.

Incredibly after these experiences, according to a psychologist, Ken Ring, a consistent set of value and belief changes take place.

> Among these changes one finds a greater appreciation for life, higher self-esteem, greater compassion for others, less concern for acquiring material wealth, a heightened sense of purpose and self-understanding, desire to learn, elevated spirituality, greater ecological sensitivity and planetary concern, and a feeling of being more intuitive.[29]

If only we all could get a glimpse of heaven and the afterlife, how different our whole world would be. And yet, could it be the hope of our gladness is right here with us now and the passage from life to death is just a door we pass through? According to Mother Teresa from her book, *A Gift for God*, we all long for heaven where God is, but we have it in our power to be in heaven with him right now--to be happy with him at this very moment. But being happy with him now means:

> loving as he loves,
> helping as he helps,
> giving as he gives,
> serving as he serves,

rescuing as he rescues,
being with him for all the twenty-four hours,
touching him in his distressing disguise."[30]

Jonathan Edwards expressed it well in a sermon, "God the Best Portion of the Christian,"

Hence we may learn, that whatever changes a godly man passes through, he is happy; because God, who is unchangeable, is his chosen portion. Though he meet with temporal losses, and be deprived of many, yea, of all his temporal enjoyments; yet God, whom he prefers before all, still remains, and cannot be lost. While he stays in this changeable, troublesome world, he is happy; because his chosen portion, on which he builds as his main foundation for happiness, is above the world, and above all changes. And when he goes into another world, still he is happy, because that portion yet remains. But how great is the happiness of those who have chosen the Fountain of all good, who prefer him before all things in heaven or on earth, and who can never be deprived of him to all eternity![31]

Is your hope in the One who remains and is with you even now? Or is your hope in what you think will gain you gladness? Don't let your expectations be in what you place your hope, be sure of what will remain after you pass from this life. Know Him, the hope of gladness, which is no less than Jesus Christ, Himself. He gave His life that we might live eternally with Him and begins the moment we trust Him for our salvation.

DAY 15

"Here's what you say to those wealthy in regard to this age! 'Don't become high and mighty or place all your hope on a gamble for riches; instead fix your hope on God, the One who richly provides everything for our enjoyment.'"
1 TIMOTHY 6:17 THE VOICE

The NIV version of the Bible says, "command those who are rich in this present world not to be arrogant nor to put their hope in wealth." Command is a strong word, but means it is a must for the wealthy believer in Christ Jesus to follow this instruction. Deuteronomy 8:18 says, "But remember the LORD your God, for it is he who gives you the ability to produce wealth…" The Lord gives the capability to make money, thereby reminding us of the provider. Indeed, the poor know it is only by the Father's hand they receive all they have. Father God reminds us that what He gives is not given that we should be arrogant about it as if we were the ones who made it, but always recognize it comes from HIs hand and be generous with all He has provided. Give to those in need and be open to whom the Father directs you to be generous. For we know not how long we will have it, so for certain, we cannot rely upon it. We can only count on God, our Father, to richly provide all we need for our enjoyment, which means for our good pleasure, getting satisfaction and benefit. Not that we should lord that pleasure over someone by thinking of ourselves more than we ought. And yet we see people flaunting their wealth all the time even though there are those that suffer from poverty every day. In fact, according to UNICEF, 22,000 children die daily from poverty. And astoundingly, "Nearly half of the world's population—more than 3 billion people—live on less than $2.50 a day."[32]

What are we doing with our money? Are we looking at our money as just for ourselves and being able to have more of it or do more with it? Are we looking for it to provide our enjoyment rather than at God to provide it? I'm sure all of us are guilty of this at one time or another, for it is the way of the world to accumulate wealth and gratify one's self and those we love. A lot of us are in debt, therefore, we don't feel we have anything to give. When I think about this, I think about the story of the widow's mite, where Jesus saw her give out of her need, rather than the others who gave out of their abundance, He said "For they all gave out of their wealth. But she, out of her poverty, put in what she had to live on, everything she had" (Mark 12:44 NET). Totally relying on God, no doubt He met her need, as He proved without fail in story after story in the Bible as well as He has in people's lives today.

Take Jon Pedley, a British millionaire, who now lives in a mud hut in Uganda. This verse fits him to a tee. He did become high and mighty from his riches, destroying everyone and everything in his path because of his insolent selfishness. During his life he encountered the Lord, but wanted to lead his own life. He pursued money above all else, only to discover, with all he had done and accomplished, he still had this hole that had not been filled. Jon says,

> "Countries like ours are full of people who have all the material comforts they desire, together with such non-material blessings as a happy family, and yet lead lives of quiet, and at some times noisy desperation, understanding nothing but the fact that there is a hole inside them and that however much food and drink they pour into it, however many motor cars and television sets they stuff it with, however many well-balanced children and loyal friends they parade around the edges of it..........it aches."[33]

This hole eventually got filled with Christ and Jon became a new man. In 2010, deciding to emulate a friend, he sold a 1.5 million dollar farmhouse in England as well as all of his businesses, literally giving it all away to start a charity in Uganda to help local orphans. But it wasn't just for the locals, British children with a troubled past were sent there to help with the locals that they, in turn, might better themselves. He said he stopped chasing money and started serving God, trying to make this bruised, broken world a better place. Jon says,

> "I now try to live my life in a way that pleases Him – and all my relationships are better, stronger and truer. I was SO scared about becoming a Christian! I was convinced that I'd become an 'un-person!' That I'd somehow be less – now I look back and can't believe how black and white my old life was next to the fantastic, Technicolor experience of knowing God and living how He made me to live. Now I have finally given my life to God I have found out that it is an experience that is full of joy."[34]

This verse today for the wealthy is not so that they miss out on the good life, it is so they will live it. And who are the wealthy? The wealthy this verse is talking about is those with more than they need, who can give so that others might not suffer. Only the joy of the Lord can cause you to exchange a 1.5 million dollar home and a life that only wealth can buy for the beauty of a mud hut in Uganda helping to make a difference in lives everyday. I'm telling you this life is about more than we can possibly conceive. God is all the wealth we need. We just have to fix, put our attention unwaveringly on Him and not on our own riches, and He will provide everything for our enjoyment and guide us into living a life beyond our wildest dreams.

DAY 16

"The LORD is good to those whose hope is in him,
to the one who seeks him;"
LAMENTATIONS 3:25

This is an unexpected verse coming from the book of Lamentations. This book in the Bible is made up of five poems each lamenting the desolation of Jerusalem in 586 B.C. Let's just say it's not a fun book to read if you are looking for something uplifting, and yet right in the middle of the book are five verses that speak of hope and the goodness of the Lord.

> Yet this I call to mind and therefore I have hope: Because of the LORD'S great love we are not consumed, for his compassions never fail. They are new every morning; great is your faithfulness. I say to myself, 'The LORD is my portion; therefore I will wait for him.' The LORD is good to those whose hope is in him, to the one who seeks him; it is good to wait quietly for the salvation of the LORD (Lamentations 3:21-26).

Right before these verses, the author, who they believe to be Jeremiah, talks about remembering his affliction and his downcast soul. And then he goes into these verses of beautiful adoration unto our King, our Lord and God. There must have been great encouragement within his spirit as he recalled this to mind. Isn't this like us? Sometimes we may be going through the worst ordeal, remembering the pain until our soul physically hurts and then for the believer, our soul reminds us of who He is, how much He cares for us and is always there. Some versions of the Bible use the word mercies instead of compassions and many of us have heard, "His mercies are new every morning," of which most of us are grateful. When the bad days come, we are so glad we can begin again the next day and know that His mercy is there waiting on us.

Of all the books in the Bible we don't look forward to reading, this one probably makes the list. And yet, this beautiful reminder of His faithfulness is something so many of us have leaned on in times of trouble. It reminds us, that this too shall pass and God will get us through. Of course, just reading the words "great is thy faithfulness" reminds me of the hymn by the same name.

Thomas Chisholm, the writer of "Great is Thy Faithfulness" was born in 1866 in a log cabin in Franklin, Kentucky. Never getting past an elementary education, he became a teacher at that same school at the age of 16. At 21, he became associate editor of his local newspaper. Thomas became a Christian at the age of 27 during a revival of Dr. Henry Clay Morrison, who persuaded him to work for him as editor of Pentecostal Herald. At the age of 36, he became a Methodist minister, but had to resign a year later due to poor health. Thomas relocated his family to Indiana to physically recover and then onto New Jersey where he became an insurance salesman for the rest of his life, not retiring until he was 87. By the time of his retirement he had written 1,200 poems, 800 of which were published. In 1923, Thomas wrote the lyrics to "Great is Thy Faithfulness" as a poem and sent it to his friend, Rev. William H. Runyan, along with several other poems. Runyan, a musician with Moody Bible Institute said, "This particular poem held such an appeal that I prayed most earnestly that my tune might carry over its message in a worthy way, and the subsequent history of its use indicates that God answered prayer."[35]

It soon became a favorite of the President of Moody Bible Institute and he decided to call an unknown singer at the time by the name of George Beverly Shea to sing it on the school's radio program. Shea then sang it at Billy Graham Crusades and the hymn gained worldwide popularity. When asked where he got the inspiration for the hymn, Thomas said, "My income has not been large at any time due to impaired health in the earlier years which has followed me on until now. Although I must not fail to record here the unfailing faithfulness of a covenant-keeping God and that He has given me many wonderful displays of His providing care, for which I am filled with astonishing gratefulness."[36]

This particular set of verses kept a man in frail health, without much education, without much income, who did an ordinary job for 37 years, "in tune" with the Lord. He knew that which sustained him and Thomas wrote out his praise in poetic form. God was so good to Thomas because he knew the One in which to place his hope. Wait quietly, seek Him and He will be your hope.

> Great is Thy faithfulness, O God my Father;
> There is no shadow of turning with Thee,
> Thou changest not, Thy compassions they fail not,
> As Thou hast been, Thou forever wilt be.
>
> Great is Thy faithfulness!
> Great is Thy faithfulness!
> Morning by morning new mercies I see
> All I have needed Thy hand hath provided
> Great is Thy faithfulness, Lord unto me!
>
> Summer and winter and springtime and harvest,
> Sun, moon, and stars in their courses above;
> Join with all nature in manifold witness,
> To Thy great faithfulness, mercy, and love.
>
> Pardon for sin and a peace that endureth,
> Thine own dear presence to cheer and to guide;
> Strength for today, and bright hope for tomorrow
> Blessings all mine, with ten thousand beside.
>
> –Thomas Chisholm

DAY 17

"Surely there is a future,
and your hope will not be cut off."
PROVERBS 23:18 ESV

One of my favorite sayings is, "Grow old along with me;
the best is yet to come." It reminds me the best years
are not behind us, but ahead. In today's culture where youth
is king, it's hard to imagine this could be true. But even the
Bible speaks of the future as being greater than what we are
experiencing now. The verse before this one and connected
with it in the Bible, speaks of not being envious of sinners,
but always be zealous, passionately devoted, to the Lord.
He knows our time here is temporary, along with all it
offers, and so our hope is not in the things this world has to
offer, but in what is to come in the next. Every day we are
immersed in the culture and bombarded by the offerings of
the world. Envy can be obvious or underlying our desires.
When our focus becomes more about what we don't have
or is on ourselves and how we don't measure up, that is a
sign we are not passionate about our pursuit of the Lord and

the future He has for us. And it is so easy to slip into envy when the same attitude is all around you.

How do we stay focused on our future hope? How do we not allow the culture around us to infect us with desires we know will only lead to envy, jealousy, and despair? For one thing, we have to be intentional, saturating our lives with more of Him than we allow of the worldly influence. God is always a gentleman. Although He pursues you and woos you with His love, He allows you to make all the decisions about what type of relationship you want with Him. His love is there, it's our love that develops as we get to know Him. So often we think we know Him when we don't. Just because we know of someone, doesn't mean we actually know him. Relationships take time, what we all seem to have so little of today. The things we deal with in life may come at us at a faster pace, but relationships can't be hurried. When we work on finding out who God is and the future He has for us, our focus doesn't become about what we don't have, or what others have, but in what He has for us. Granted we see lives all the time sold out for Christ that we think we wouldn't want to emulate or do what they do, but then again we are comparing our lives to someone else. We are each unique and the future He has for us is custom made for our life, for no two lives are exactly alike.

Envy has long been around since the beginning of man. We see it in the story of Cain killing his brother Abel because of God's favor on his brother's offering over his own, but even before that with Eve. She listened to the serpent, the devil himself, and believed if she ate the fruit from the Tree of Good and Evil, she could be as wise as God. She envied what God had that she believed He was holding back from her. And we do the same thing every time we envy what someone else has that we don't. We believe God is holding out on us instead of trusting Him to give us what is best. Envy is considered one of the "Seven Deadly Sins" recognized by the church based off of Proverbs 6:16-19 and found later on in Galatians 5:19-21. Envy can also directly be related to the 10th commandment, "Thou shalt not covet..." Some other verses that speak on envy are as follows:

> But if you have bitter jealousy and selfish ambition in your hearts, do not boast and be false to the truth. This is not the wisdom that comes down from above, but is earthly, unspiritual, demonic. For where jealousy and selfish ambition exist, there will be disorder and every vile practice (James 3:14-16 ESV).

> A tranquil heart gives life to the flesh, but envy makes the bones rot (Proverbs 14:30 ESV).

Nothing speaks of a bad future like our bones rotting. The people I have known to be "green with envy," as the saying goes, are sick. Also, if being envious is associated with the demonic, disorder and every vile practice, nothing in that promises a future.

According to a *New York Post* article on October 27, 2013, Mingdong Chen, 25, an illegal immigrant, butchered unmercifully, his cousin's family over bitter envy, killing the wife, three young children, and a baby. The husband of the murdered family had invited his cousin to live with them until he could establish himself and live the American dream. But instead, envy caused him to do an unspeakable act to his own blood relatives.

He "showed no remorse when he confessed to slaughtering the family that allowed him to live in their Brooklyn apartment and admitted he committed the atrocity because he envied their way of life, a police source told *The Post*. "The family had too much," the source quoted Chen as saying. "He meant that the family had better income and a better lifestyle than him ... He was jealous and just killed them."[37]

Don't let envy consume you. Don't even entertain it before it embeds itself in your soul and leads to something worse. Trust the Father with your future; He is the hope you can be sure of to work everything out for your good.

DAY 18

*"For I know the thoughts that I think toward you,
says the LORD, thoughts of peace and not of evil,
to give you a future and a hope."*
JEREMIAH 29:11 NKJV

This verse is probably one of the most beloved verses in the Bible. Believers often hang onto it when there seems to be no hope, and it provided hope for the Israelites to cling to while they were in captivity in Babylon. When all around you looks bleak, it's comforting to know God is thinking about you and has some plans in place for your future. So often in our times of stagnation, where we feel we are not moving at all, where we don't know how to get out of what we have gotten ourselves into, or where we are still, and it's not where we would like to be, we stop living. It's like we don't know how to move forward because the direction we were going in brought us to this place. Instead of looking at it like it is for a season and seeking the Lord, we are paralyzed by fear. We seek out friends, mentors and those in authority over us, in hopes that they will tell us what we want to hear. We just want to get out of this place where we are held in bondage, whether it be an actual place, our physical body, or an emotional cell.

God says in the following verses, "'You will seek me and find me when you seek me with all your heart. I will be found by you,' declares the LORD 'and will bring you back from captivity'" (Jeremiah 29:13-14a).

Sounds like there was a reason for the captivity. The Israelites had fallen far from God and had gone their own way. Following everyone and everything but Him. That was why they were so easily captured and now found themselves in exile, in a foreign land. The Lord knew it would take a while before they were ready to go back to the Promised Land He had given them. He knew being held captive by the enemy, doesn't just happen overnight and you have to get free in your mind and soul before you are free in your body. In fact, in verses Jeremiah 29:5-7, the Lord tells them,

> Build houses and settle down; plant gardens and eat what they produce. Marry and have sons and daughters; find wives for your sons and give your daughters in marriage, so that they too may have sons and daughters. Increase in number there; do not decrease. Also, seek the peace and prosperity of the city to which I have carried you into exile. Pray to the LORD for it, because if it prospers, you too will prosper.

They did not like where they were, but the Lord was definitely letting them know they were going to be there for a while. "Live," He said, "live." So often we want to die when we get in these places. Dying seems like the easy way out and living seems too hard. But seeking the Lord with our whole hearts is what helps us to live. It frees us to see things differently and trust Him with the outcome. Not only did He tell them to live, He told them to seek the peace and prosperity of the city they were living in, the city of their captor, their enemy. For in their prayers they would receive the same benefit.

I have met so many people that just exist. They are like leaves carried in the wind allowing life to take them wherever, yet dead where they are. They have so many regrets about how life hasn't turned out like they planned; they can't live the lives they have. Their focus is on something far in the future and therefore, they never put roots down where they are. They don't engage in the community they have been planted in and instead of praying over it for peace and prosperity, they speak over it negatively, comparing it to where they came from or some other place they would rather be. They are afraid if they embrace where they are and trust God for their future, somehow this will tarnish or take away from where they want to be. And yet God says in His Word, "From one man he made all the nations, that they should inhabit the whole earth; and he marked out their appointed times in history and the boundaries of their lands" (Acts 17:26).

When we started moving because of my husband's job, it was tough. We had already moved ourselves into three rentals in eighteen months, but now the company needed to move us to another state. We had just had our first baby and she was only four months old. At least they packed us up, loaded, and moved us. All we had to do was get in the car and drive. But as any of you know who have had children, they can be a job by themselves. As if that wasn't enough, the day they loaded all of our worldly goods, it was snowing, a rarity for Hartsville, South Carolina. We were moving to the big city of Atlanta, Georgia, and I was excited to be moving to a big town. We had to meet with the realtor as soon as we got to the hotel. Our household stuff was going into storage until we could find our new home. We were running late getting to the hotel, so as soon as we got there, the realtor was in the parking lot waiting. I grabbed everything I thought I needed for our baby and me and we all headed out. When we returned, our car windows were smashed and I realized my purse as well as a cooler bag had been stolen. I thought I grabbed all of that when we left, but with a baby in tow, sometimes it's hard to remember what you have. I was devastated, exhausted, and mad. I had thrown every last minute valuable thing I had from moving into that purse, including all our recent Christmas photos and the only home movie of my brother and me as children, and now it was gone.

Being uprooted from a place can be difficult. You don't always get to take everything with you, things get lost, and friends and favorite places are left behind. We quite often wish we could just go home where it seems safe, easy, and comfortable, but that's not always in the cards for lots of different reasons. You can either regroup and plunge in or sit back and be depressed. God's way is to settle in for the long haul. He's got the future, but He needs you to live in the now.

I've lived in 15 different houses in 30 years of marriage. Needless to say there were many more moves after that one. During that time I had another child and all that comes with everyday life. Instead of waiting at each place to get to our final destination, we treated each place like a vacation and enjoyed everything in that area. At first, it wasn't easy, but I had to learn to adjust and trust the Father for the outcome. Looking back on my life so far, I am eternally grateful for the plan God had for me. I can see each place, the people in my life there and the distinct season it was in my spiritual life. I don't know what's ahead, but I know my sweet Father God has it all planned out.

DAY 19

"We have this hope as an anchor for the soul, firm and secure. It enters the inner sanctuary behind the curtain,"
HEBREWS 6:19

What is the anchor to your soul? Is it your spouse, your children, your house? What is the thing or person in which you put your hope, which you count immovable, sure, and steady? If you answer none of these things and say it is Jesus, would others know that by the life you live? Do they see evidence in your actions and your speech that He is the source of your steadiness, stability and grounding? Do you constantly refer back to Him as the reason for your hope and give Him the glory for being the constant presence in your life and always looking out for you? These are questions to ask ourselves to be sure about what is keeping us from really drifting in this life. Otherwise, there will be things and people we have as an anchor for a season, time, or perhaps our entire life, placing them in a position that only God can fill.

Life can be hard and quite often we don't understand why some things happen to us. Instead of looking to God, we look to others and things to give us the answers, something we can hang onto, when we feel like we are drowning or falling into something we can't control. But where is God in all this? If He is our intermediary between heaven and earth, don't we think He can handle anything we are dealing with?

In the previous verse, before Hebrews 6:19, it says when we take hold of this hope we are greatly encouraged. We can know that in this life He is firm and secure and has us no matter what happens. We no longer need to go to someone else or a priest with our problems, we can go straight to Him.

On the day of the crucifixion, Jesus made that clear by the veil (curtain) in front of the Holy of Holies in the Temple being torn in two from top to bottom the moment He died. Indeed this was no ordinary curtain, it was 60 feet long, 30 feet wide and according to the Talmud was a handbreadth in thickness approximately four inches thick. Also, according to Rabbinic tradition, it took 300 priests to handle it for cleaning when it became soiled. No doubt no ordinary man could have torn it asunder. Other signs also happened that day to prove He indeed was the Son of God. There was an eclipse for three hours, an earthquake, and tombs broke open of many dead, holy people, who came back to life. They walked into the holy city and appeared to many after His resurrection.

> When the centurion and those with him who were guarding Jesus saw the earthquake and all that had happened, they were terrified, and exclaimed 'Surely he was the Son of God!' (Matthew 27:54).

God didn't want there to be any question about what Jesus's sacrifice was about. It was about redemption and love.

Jesus's blood paid the price for our sins that we might have access to the Father through Him. He is the only way to fellowship with the Father, Son, and Holy Spirit. He is the solid rock on which we can stand and anchors us to be unwavering in our faith. It is interesting to note that early period boat anchors were rocks. Which I believe was what the writer of Hebrews wants us to grasp in this scripture visual.

Edward Mote, a young man, left to his own devices and who had no Christian upbringing, became an apprentice to a Christian carpenter and learned the ways of the Lord. On the way to work one day, thinking about the Parable of the Wise and Foolish Builders in the Bible, found in Matthew 7:24-27, he felt inspired to write down a verse. Edward loved worship music, and before the day was over, he had written four stanzas. Not long after this, he was visiting a friend whose wife was deathly ill. It was Sunday, so his friend said they liked to honor it by singing a hymn, reading a scripture, and having prayer together. Edward remembered the hymn he had in his pocket, so they sang it together. His friend's wife liked it so much she requested a copy of it for herself. Encouraged by her interest, Edward made 1000 copies and gave them to friends. His song "My Hope is Built on Nothing Less" was published in 1837.

> My hope is built on nothing less
> Than Jesus' blood and righteousness;
> I dare not trust the sweetest frame,
> But wholly lean on Jesus' name.
> On Christ, the solid Rock, I stand;
> All other ground is sinking sand.

When darkness veils His lovely face,
I rest on His unchanging grace;
In every high and stormy gale
My anchor holds within the veil.
On Christ, the solid Rock, I stand;
All other ground is sinking sand.

His oath, His covenant, and blood
Support me in the whelming flood;
When every earthly prop gives way,
He then is all my Hope and Stay.
On Christ, the solid Rock, I stand;
All other ground is sinking sand.

When He shall come with trumpet sound,
Oh, may I then in Him be found,
Clothed in His righteousness alone,
Faultless to stand before the throne!
On Christ, the solid Rock, I stand;
All other ground is sinking sand.

-Edward Mote

When you look at the words to this hymn, you can see truly Edward Mote knew the rock, "the anchor" in which he put his hope. The one who could connect him with the Father, who longed for him to be in His Presence. As a carpenter, he gave up a very lucrative business as a cabinet-maker to become a preacher at the age of 55. He decided that showing people what to build upon for their futures was more important than what they might need on earth today.

DAY 20

"Yes, my soul, find rest in God;
my hope comes from him."
PSALM 62.5

What gives you rest? Because of the intensity and pace of life, many find they cannot find rest. We often think of rest as sleep, but it can also mean relaxation, downtime, a vacation, or ceasing from strenuous or stressful activity. In this particular Psalm, David is tired, tired of lies and assaults, reminding himself to rest in the Lord, to trust Him for the outcome of his life. It can be hard when you feel others are against you, hurting you, or lying about you. You want to hurt them back, but you know the outcome of that is never good. Trusting in the Father to take care of all of your needs can be difficult when you feel capable, physically, mentally, or emotionally. But that is what the Christian life is all about, giving our lives over to Him. We hand over our natural rights to react and seek out the Father in prayer, trusting Him to answer. Even when He seems silent, we know that means we must patiently wait.

In Israel, as well as the ancient Near East, the word shepherd was a widely used metaphor for kings. The Lord is often called the Shepherd of Israel. David, being a former shepherd, knew well what that meant in how the Father cared for us, His sheep. He spoke of it so beautifully in the 23rd Psalm, which has given so many comforts. There is a reason for the verse, "He maketh me to lie down in green pastures…" (Psalm 23:2 KJV)

But few of us know what a shepherd does if his sheep need rest. Phillip Keller in his book, *A Shepherd Looks at Psalm 23* says because of their makeup there are four reasons why it is impossible for sheep to rest or lie down.

1. Because of their timidity, they must be free from all fear.

2. Because of their social makeup within their flock, there must be no friction among their kind.

3. If tormented by flies or parasites, they cannot rest until free from these pests.

4. They must be completely free from hunger and not feel the need to find food.[38]

Wow, there is a reason we are compared to sheep, we are so much like them in our behavior. While walking on a road in Ireland one day, I came upon a flock of sheep. Just the rocks crunching under my feet startled them and caused them to jump and begin to run. I stopped in my tracks and saw them staring at me full of fear. I simply wanted to take their picture, yet I was only allowed to get so close. Talk about on edge! With sheep, the slightest movement can cause them to run. The other sheep with them will run with the one frightened, not even bothering to find out the cause. Sheep are feeble creatures so they see their only recourse is to run. But when the shepherd is there, they feel safe and know he is watching over them.

Anxiety can be another word for fear and in today's society it is becoming widespread and is even termed a disorder, for some requiring medication. I wonder how many of those that are highly anxiety driven realize that the Great Shepherd is watching over them. That He is looking out for their good and will take care of their needs.

> For God hath not given us the spirit of fear;
> but of power, and of love, and of a sound mind
> (2 Timothy 1:7 KJV).

A sound mind is not one full of fear or concern about what is to come. If God gave us a spirit of love, power and a sound mind, then we should not be startled by what comes or moved, but should look to the Great Shepherd to guide us in every way. Living in this way, will let us rest, no matter what is going on around us.

> In peace I will both lie down and sleep, For You
> alone, O LORD, make me to dwell in safety
> (Psalm 4:8 NASB).

Sheep like people and other animals have a hierarchy of order. Sheep will butt, drive, and intimidate other ewes to get to better grazing ground. This behavior causes unrest, conflict, and jealousy, as the sheep never feel settled. Hanging onto or fighting for our territory robs us of rest. When the shepherd is there, all that foolishness ends as sheep recognize that only one is in charge and all the rest of them are equal. The shepherd must deal out discipline to those sheep who have been cruel, and in contrast, he shows great compassion to those who have been dealt with unmercifully by the other sheep.

> Therefore this is what the Sovereign LORD says to them: See, I myself will judge between the fat sheep and the lean sheep. Because you shove with flank and shoulder, butting all the weak sheep with your horns until you have driven them away, I will save my flock, and they will no longer be plundered. I will judge between one sheep and another (Ezekiel 34:20-22).

Rest and contentment only comes when we know the Great Shepherd is in charge. We trust where He has placed us and who He has allowed to shepherd us here on earth. We sense and live in His presence and know ultimately He is the one we answer to, finding great contentment and rest for our souls.

Sheep cannot rest when different types of flies and ticks bite them in the summer. They will move and shake their heads trying to get free. A good shepherd daily watching over each of his sheep will notice when they are bothered by these parasites and will apply the necessary repellents and insect dips. He will find places of shelter for them where they can find refuge from these pests. The irritations of life do the same for us. Torment by the enemy can be disguised as thoughts and deeds. Only when we allow the balm of the Holy Spirit being applied by our Savior can we find contentment and rest.

The Lord promised the Israelites a land full of milk and honey, which in farming terms, means that it was lush. Hunger would not be a problem, but they would have to follow his lead to get to it. Sheep, in a good pasture, can be 100 pounds in weight 100 days from birth, resting and ruminating. Because many of the lands where sheep graze are dry and semi-arid countries, the shepherd must work the land to prepare good grazing area for his sheep. Plowing, planting, removing rocks, roots and stumps, irrigation, seeding, and planting are just some of the things necessary to prepare green pasture for sheep to graze on. Just like in our lives there is so much the Good Shepherd has to do with our hearts, minds, and souls to prepare us to receive the good things He has for us. When we follow him, He will work all things out for us to be able to receive, not be hungry, and rest in knowing He will meet all our needs.

Our Savior, in whom we place our hope, is such a Good Shepherd, and we, like sheep must follow Him in order to find our rest.

DAY 21

*"And everyone who has this hope fixed on Him
purifies himself, just as He is pure."*
1 JOHN 3:3 NASB

Purity in the Old Testament of the Bible is focused on ritual purification through cleansing and in the New Testament the focus is righteousness through the finished work of Christ. John is not saying this is something we have to achieve on our own; this can only be accomplished through Christ Jesus. He states in the previous verses we are God's children and God lavishes His love upon us. And then says this before our verse for today: "...now we are children of God, and what we will be has not yet been made known. But we know that when He appears, we shall be like him, for we shall see him as he is" (1 John 3:2).

When we, as God's children, knowing that we are lavishly loved, are permanently settled on Christ Jesus as our hope, and He lives in us, then He will purify us as He is pure. In other words, we will become more and more like him each day. He will guide us to do what is right. "No one who is born of God will continue to sin, because God's seed remains in them; they cannot go on sinning, because they have been born of God" (1 John 3:9).

When we are born of God, we will no longer desire to sin against Him because He now lives within us through the Holy Spirit, changing our desires into desires to live righteously through Him. When we receive Him into our lives, that great love with which He loves us, will pour out through us to others more and more. Of course, it won't all happen at once, because

> For our struggle is not against flesh and blood, but against the rulers, against the authorities, against the powers of this dark world and against the spiritual forces of evil in the heavenly realms (Ephesians 6:12).

The struggle is real, but we have hope in the One, who defeated our foe and his band of evil forces, by dying on the cross. His love for us and our belief in Jesus Christ, is what takes us over the finish line. What separates us from the world and the children of the evil one is our love for others, which must be shown in both actions and truth.

In our verse today, purify means to be cleansed from defilement, anything that makes us unholy, before the Lord. We know naturally within each of ourselves what is morally right and what is morally wrong. That is why most of the laws which are established in the governments of the world, follow what was given to us by God, as the Ten Commandments. The good thing is we have an advocate in

Christ, who can purify us, helping us do the right thing and bringing others into His kingdom by our example.

As Solomon says, "there is nothing new under the sun" in Ecclesiastes 1:9. We've learned nothing from history and continue to make the same mistakes. We have times of morality and times of rebellion, and even though we know something of recent history, we seem to be ignorant of the moral mistakes of others in the past. No society which is cognizant of loving others as they love themselves collapses, for they are all looking out for the good of one another and therefore they are a united front against any enemy. When a society becomes focused on self, not looking to God, then, "Having lost all sensitivity, they have given themselves over to sensuality so as to indulge in every kind of impurity, and they are full of greed" (Ephesians 4:19).

Sound familiar? Not unlike any time before, since time began really, just sad in light of what we could be. Many have found the way through Jesus, living lives of purity and leading others to Him. Some have even been martyred for their faith, for being pure in their devotion to Christ. Considering death the better option over allowing something to stain the pureness of Christ in them. Purity in Christ is so much more than lack of sexual sin or other immoral degrading thoughts. However prudish, modern society may think purity is, it brings health to our spirit, mind and body.

Blessed are the pure in heart: for they will see God (Matthew 5:8 KJV).

Some who have gone before us had this to say about purity: "God would not rub so hard if it were not to fetch out the dirt that is ingrained in our natures. God loves purity so well He had rather see a hole than a spot in His child's garments." –William Gurnal

"If thou hadst simplicity and purity, thou wouldst be able to comprehend all things without error, and behold them without danger. The pure heart safely pervades not only heaven, but hell." –Thomas A Kempis

"He came to deliver us from our sinful dispositions, and create in us pure hearts, and when we have Him with us it will not be hard for us. Then the service of Christ will be delightful." –Dwight L. Moody

Finally, brothers and sisters, whatever is true, whatever is noble, whatever is right, whatever is pure, whatever is lovely, whatever is admirable—if anything is excellent or praiseworthy—think about such things. And the God of peace will be with you (Philippians 4:8, 9b). –Paul, an apostle of Christ

I look forward to the day when Christ's kingdom is established; it truly will be like nothing we have ever seen. Evil will be abolished and truth and purity will reign. Until then we are to keep our hope fixed on Him, letting Him purify us as He is pure.

DAY 22

"Why are you cast down, O my soul? And why are you disquieted within me? Hope in God, for I shall yet praise Him For the help of His countenance."
PSALM 42:5,11, 43:5 NKJV

This same verse is repeated three times as stated above and in many Hebrew manuscripts, these two psalms are one. This verse begins with a question of why is his soul bowed down to him, why is it murmuring within him. Haven't we all been there at one time or another? Grief or depression can usually cause our souls to be at a place of utter despair, not knowing how to come out of it, desperate for someone to help us. The psalmist here knows that is where he is and is asking himself these questions, wondering how he could even feel this way, knowing he knows the Lord and the beauty of His presence. He states in the Psalm that he would be leading others going to church with shouts of joy and thanksgiving, so excited was he to meet with the Lord. He knows his despair is affecting other men's opinions about the God he serves because they see him in this state, they are asking where is his God now. Not a good witness of the joy of the Lord that is for sure and he knows it. That is why he is crying out for that deep intimacy with the Lord that he knows it takes to give him joy that overcomes his circumstances, his feelings. Intimacy with the Lord that is as refreshing as a waterfall and as powerful as a wave breaking over him.

When you know the Lord in that way, it can be incredibly frustrating when you are overcome with feelings of grief, depression, or despair. You know He's got this, He directs His love by day over you and at night, Job 35:10 says He "gives songs in the night." What more could we ask for than the Lord's 24-hour care concerning us? The psalmist knows this and is reminding himself of the goodness of his Lord. Periods of time when we are assaulted with grief or depression we can't seem to shake, we have to remember who God is, how He cares for us and praise Him for the hope that He is and provides concerning all our circumstances. He knew what was coming and wants to provide you comfort and joy in the midst, yet we must allow Him to enter our presence with His Presence. Only in His Presence can we experience the fullness of joy.

> You will make known to me the path of life; In Your Presence is fullness of joy; In Your right hand there are pleasures forever (Psalm 16:11 NASB).

"It is Well with My Soul," a favorite Christian hymn was written by Horatio Gates Spafford at a very grievous time in his life. He was a well-known lawyer in Chicago in the 1860s and he and his wife, Anna, were well-known and prominent supporters and friends with D.L. Moody. In 1871 Horatio invested in enormous tracts of land north of Chicago, which was expanding. When the Great Fire of Chicago burned down the city that same year, it also destroyed much of his investment. Then scarlet fever took his four-year-old son from him. Two years later, in 1873, he decided his family should go on holiday to Europe, knowing that fall D. L. Moody would be preaching there. His wife and their four daughters, Annie age 11, Maggie age 9, Bessie age 5, and Tanetta age 2, would go ahead of him by ship since he still had to take care of some business. Then the unthinkable happened, another ship struck their ship, and 226 people lost their lives, including all four of their daughters. Anna managed to survive and upon arriving in England sent Horatio a telegram with the words "Saved alone." Horatio then set sail for England passing over the location where his daughters tragically died and wrote the beloved hymn we all know as "It is Well with My Soul."

> When peace, like a river, attendeth my way,
> When sorrows like sea billows roll;
> Whatever my lot, Thou hast taught me to say,
> It is well, it is well with my soul.
>
> (Refrain:) It is well (it is well),
> with my soul (with my soul),
> It is well, it is well with my soul.
>
> Though Satan should buffet, though trials should come,

Let this blest assurance control,
That Christ hath regarded my helpless estate,
And hath shed His own blood for my soul.

My sin, oh the bliss of this glorious thought!
My sin, not in part but the whole,
Is nailed to His cross, and I bear it no more,
Praise the Lord, praise the Lord, O my soul!

For me, be it Christ, be it Christ hence to live:
If Jordan above me shall roll,
No pain shall be mine, for in death as in life
Thou wilt whisper Thy peace to my soul.

And Lord haste the day, when the faith shall be sight,
The clouds be rolled back as a scroll;
The trump shall resound, and the Lord shall descend,
Even so, it is well with my soul.

-Horatio Spafford

Most of us have difficulty surviving one difficult time or tragedy in our lives, much less this many and of this magnitude. Obviously Horatio Spafford knew his Lord and knew Him well. He knew God was his only hope and in Him was the only means by which he would be able to survive the difficulties he would face in this life. Of course he had his time of grief, but he chose to look to the Father to supply the joy and strength he knew he needed to go on.

And go on he did. Horatio and Anna, in time, had three more children, his second and only other son died of scarlet fever at three. After suffering their tragic losses, Anna, Horatio, and their children decided to move to Jerusalem and help others there, calling themselves the American Colony. Some viewed them as a sort of Christian utopian society, but their philanthropic efforts did much to aid the people there and the Spafford Children's Center, established by their daughter, Bertha, is in operation today providing healthcare for disadvantaged and vulnerable children in need.

Whatever you are going through, Christ Jesus can bring you through it. Look to Him, remembering all His benefits and know that even if the difficulty seems never to end, we can know He is there waiting with a brighter future we can look forward to. For what He has already done on the cross is enough to be worthy of our praise. He is our hope and it is in our praise that we will receive our joy.

DAY 23

*"Now faith is confidence in what we hope for and
assurance about what we do not see."*
HEBREWS 11:1

I love it! The biblical definition of faith is right here. The
confidence in what we hope for is faith and it is the assurance of what we do not see. What are you confident about
or confident in that is yet to come or that you cannot see?
Faith is not logical in a worldly sense, but is absolutely
foundational in a biblical sense. This chapter is called the
"Hall of Faith" in the Bible and lists great men, women, creation and things that happened because of faith. It encour-
ages us, spurs us on, and ignites the spark of belief within
us. We exhibit faith everyday, whether we recognize it or
not, when we ride in a car, plane, elevator, or amusement
ride, expect the sun to rise and set, even that we will wake
up and expect life to go on. We truly live by faith and yet so
often we cannot see that we do, whether we are religious or
not. We think everything is absolute and concrete, when in
fact, most things are discovered by believing in the unseen,

hoping in an idea or concept that seems unbelievable to others. Faith has brought about some of our greatest inventions and scientific discoveries, believing in something long before we see it. Like Edison with the phonograph, light bulb, and moving pictures or Henry Ford with the first automobile. Our future will look very different from our present as more and more discoveries prove what has been believed by faith will become fact.

As far as the Bible is concerned, many consider the miracle of the Red Sea parting for the Israelites to cross in order to escape the Egyptian army, just an allegory to increase one's faith. And yet it has been discovered only recently that this feat could have been accomplished. One theory is presented here:

> Drews and oceanographer Weiqing Han analyzed archaeological records, satellite measurements and current-day maps to estimate the water-flow and depth that could have existed 3,000 years ago. They then used an ocean computer model to simulate the impact of an overnight wind at that site.

> "The results were that a wind of 63 mph, lasting for 12 hours, would have pushed back waters estimated to be six feet deep. That would have exposed mudflats for four hours, creating a dry passage about 2 to 2.5 miles long and 3 miles wide. As soon as the wind stopped, the waters would come rushing back," UCAR said.

"There are a number of details (in Exodus) like the duration of the wind and the direction of the wind that support the computer model," Drews said. "The fact that bodies washed up on the Eastern shore where the Israelites were able to see them — details like that were confirmed by the ocean model."

"From a theological standpoint, the timing of the Red Sea parting when Moses and his people needed to cross shows the miracle," Drews said. "From a faith perspective, it has always made sense to me that God uses natural action to carry out his plan if he so chooses," said Drews.[39]

Some need scientific proof before they can believe, but that's not faith. Faith is belief in what we can't see based on the truth of God. It's knowing what He says in His Word is true, trusting Him and living it out. Many in the Old Testament of the Bible believed in the Messiah to come, Jesus Christ, and their faith was counted unto them as righteousness. We, as believers, after the time of Christ, believe He has come, died, and rose again, and we believe all that the Word of God has to say about Him. I would rather serve a God of the impossible than place my hope in only what man can do and provide.

Immediately following this great hall of faith chapter, the very next verse in Hebrews 12:1 says, "Therefore, since we are surrounded by such a great cloud of witnesses, let us throw off everything that hinders and the sin that so easily entangles. And let us run with perseverance the race marked out for us."

Run the race! Those that have gone before us are cheering us on! The race is already marked out for us, let nothing stop us from continuing on, knowing the win is already assured by the victory that took place on the cross. Death was defeated and eternal life with God was won. This is our faith, believe it, receive it, and reseed it in others. For soon we will join that great cloud of witnesses and cheer those who come behind us on to victory in Christ. Put your hope in the One that you can be fully confident will reveal what you cannot see.

DAY 24

"And hope does not put us to shame, because God's love has been poured out into our hearts through the Holy Spirit, who has been given to us."
ROMANS 5:5

In the verses leading up to this one, Paul is explaining why and when we should rejoice. We certainly should rejoice in our justification through faith and our peace in God and the hope of His glory. But we should also rejoice when we go through sufferings because we know "...that suffering produces perseverance; perseverance, character; and character, hope" (Romans 5:3-4). And in this hope we will not be put to shame, for God will surely be with us and His love that has been poured in us through the Holy Spirit will bring us through whatever we must endure.

Now suffering can be minor everyday problems, grievances or more difficult and complex issues. Suffering in the biblical definition can mean the bearing of pain, inconvenience, or loss. I'm sure all of us can attest to imperfect days, where something will inevitably cause some type of suffering. Most of us tend to rationalize our suffering by comparing it to the pain of others, feeling guilty at times for even being concerned about it. But do we rejoice about it? Do we see it as advantageous for our growth in Christ? Do we realize that as we get through it or endure it, it is producing in us the beauty of Christ's image? Sometimes it is as simple as your day didn't go as well as expected or you let the weather affect your mood. Sometimes it is more devastating such as your home has been destroyed, when you lose a loved one, when you've been hurt in a car wreck that wasn't your fault, these and so many other things can cause us to moan and complain about the unfairness and difficulties of life. Obviously, we will have our moments of shock, grief, sadness, anger, and disappointment, etc., but knowing God's got this, those should be short-lived, directing our attention to Him and not the circumstances. Paul, the apostle, certainly knew about suffering. He states the following in 2 Corinthians 11:24-28 NLT:

> "Five different times the Jewish leaders gave me thirty-nine lashes. Three times I was beaten with rods. Once I was stoned. Three times I was shipwrecked. Once I spent a whole night and a day adrift at sea. I have traveled on many long journeys. I have faced danger from rivers and from robbers. I have faced danger from my own people, the Jews, as well as from the Gentiles. I have faced danger in the cities, in the deserts, and on the seas. And I have faced danger from men who claim to be believers but are not. I have worked hard and long, endur-

ing many sleepless nights. I have been hungry and thirsty and have often gone without food. I have shivered in the cold, without enough clothing to keep me warm. Then, besides all this, I have the daily burden of my concern for all the churches."

The fact that none of these difficulties slowed him down in his pursuit to bring God glory and honor by continuing to proclaim the gospel, without shame or concern for himself, is powerful evidence of the Holy Spirit in him. Not only will the power of the Holy Spirit in us give us the strength to endure or overcome, the love He has poured out in our hearts will fill us with joy. Therefore, we should never be ashamed for what we must go through in life, but look at it as what is building our perseverance, character, and hope in Christ Jesus.

> Someone asked C.S. Lewis, "Why do the righteous suffer?"
>
> "Why not?" he replied. "They're the only ones who can take it."[39]

What a badge of honor, that we are the only ones who can take it! It shows others what we believe is real, worth dying for or suffering for that others might gain salvation. If we were like the world, how else would they know about eternal life? This hope will never put us to shame, for the value we gain from whatever we endure for the sake of Christ will not even compare to anything we could have gained on this earth.

DAY 25

*"Therefore, since we have such a hope,
we are very bold."*
2 CORINTHIANS 3:12

Bold is one of those words we like to use to describe food like a spicy dish or Doritos® It's not a word we like to use in describing ourselves or others, because in today's world that can come off as aggressive. We like to think of ourselves as more politically correct or tolerant of others, so there really should be no need for anyone to be bold, just let everyone make his or her choices. Then everyone is happy and there is peace. Please. There will not be total peace until Jesus's return, and the earth is restored to its intended glory. Until then, we are to be strong in our faith and bold in our proclamation of it to others. That doesn't mean forceful or pushy, just absolutely so confident in what we believe; it is unequivocally convicting to others. Are you that sure about what you believe? The Disciples were and so should Jesus's followers be.

> When they (the rulers, elders and teachers of the law) saw the boldness of Peter and John and realized that they were unschooled, ordinary men, they were astonished and recognized that they had been with Jesus (Acts 4:13 BSB).

What is the hope that can make us very bold? Not just bold, but very bold? The hope Paul is referring to in this verse is the surpassing glory of the ministry of the Spirit, far surpassing the glory that was experienced with Moses and the law. His challenge to us is to be bold in our proclamation of the gospel, which sets us free from keeping the law. God knew we couldn't keep the law perfectly that is why Jesus had to die on the cross to be the substitute lamb to take away the sins of the world, past, present and future. When we see Christ and the truth of who He is, and receive Him as our Savior, then we know within ourselves we have been forgiven and are finally set free.

> For in Christ Jesus the law of the Spirit of life has set you free from the law of sin and death (Romans 8:2 BSB).
>
> So if the Son sets you free, you will be free indeed (John 8:36).

This freedom truly sets men free. We will fight for the freedom of our country faster than we will fight for the heavenly kingdom. We will fight for our children faster than we will fight for our King. But when it all comes down to the end, if we don't know Jesus, the blessed hope, we will have missed out on the real freedom, the one that lasts for all of eternity. It is this freedom, this glorious hope that we can be completely confident and bold in sharing with others so they might be free.

Joan of Arc, even at 13, caught on early to the truth of this freedom. A peasant farm girl, she grew up in a French village, surrounded by the pro-Burgundian occupation of the villages around her, which were against the French crown. This internal strife between two factions to claim the kingship was giving the English an advantage in the Hundred Years' War over the French. The English had taken control of most of France, and it looked as if they soon would have all of it due to these divided factions. Joan, later at her trial, testified that at 13 in her father's garden she experienced her first vision of the Archangel Michael, Saint Catherine, and Saint Margaret, two Christian martyrs. They told her to drive out the English and bring the Dauphin-heir to the throne to Reims for the coronation. So at 16, she asked a relative to take her to the garrison commander to request an armed guard to take her to the royal court. His sarcastic reply at her request did not deter her from what she considered an absolute necessity. The following January, she returned and gained support from two of the soldiers there when she said, "I must be at the King's side ... there will be no help (for the kingdom) if not from me. Although I would rather have remained spinning [wool] at my mother's side ... yet must I go and must I do this thing, for my Lord wills that I do so."[40]

With the support of these two soldiers, she gained a second meeting with the garrison commander and gave him a prophetic word about a reversal in a battle several days before messengers arrived to report it. She said she received this divine revelation while tending her flock of sheep back home. This revelation was enough for the commander to get her an audience before the royal court. To journey through hostile territory, she had to be disguised as a male soldier and cut her hair.

> After arriving at the Royal Court she impressed Charles VII during a private conference. After years of one humiliating defeat after another, both the military and civil leadership of France were demoralized and discredited. Only a regime in the final straits of desperation would pay any heed to an illiterate farm girl who claimed that the voice of God was instructing her to take charge of her country's army and lead it to victory.[41]

After many victories, Joan was eventually captured by the English and had to stand trial for heresy. The trial was politically motivated, as the English had been humiliated in defeat by this young, illiterate, peasant, girl. Convicted for cross-dressing, a capital offense, Joan, only 19, was burned at the stake. So many knew she was innocent, including her executioner who feared he would be greatly damned. The Church later, at a nullification trial, found Joan of Arc innocent of all charges.

Joan first heard from the Lord at 13 and said she was much afraid. Just like us, she knew though, that the Lord required her to be bold. To share the words Joan received for the King required boldness and perseverance that would affect many lives and help to bring freedom to her country. Yes, she died a senseless death, but no one has forgotten what she did to bring about freedom for many in her pursuit to honor God. In her own words, "Since God had commanded it, it was necessary that I do it. Since God commanded it, even if I had a hundred fathers and mothers, even if I had been a King's daughter, I would have gone nevertheless."[42]

At first we can be afraid, like the Virgin Mary or many of the disciples when faced with what God asks of us, but somehow, through divine intervention, when we boldly step out in faith, and believe, through this hope of Jesus Christ as our Messiah, He fulfills what He has asked us to do. Are you boldly living in the hope to which you have been called?

DAY 26

"Therefore, prepare your minds for action; be self-controlled; set your hope fully on the grace to be given you when Jesus Christ is revealed."
1 PETER 1:13

Some versions of this scripture use the words gird up instead of prepare. In the language of the first century, gird up literally meant "to gather up your long, flowing garments and be ready for physical activity." Peter, the disciple of Jesus, was letting believers know there would be physical action involved in their call to Christ. He also said to be self-controlled, some versions say sober-minded, meaning fully awake so you can pray. Watching out for the enemy who is always looking for someone to devour, not caught up in the things or anxieties of this world such as carousing, drunkenness, and sexual immorality. Have your mind clear and on the things of Christ so you will be ready at all times. And last, but not least, set your hope on what you will receive when Christ is revealed.

It can be hard to have your mind on Jesus the whole time in church, much less all the time. Our minds are so bombarded with the things of this world, it truly is difficult to fill them with the things of God. That is why we have to be intentional in making sure we are setting aside time to be with God, both in prayer and time in His Word. If not, we can be sure the things of this world will reign in our minds. We think we need to keep up with the news and with people, but not to the neglect of our time with Christ. If we can't put Him first, then how will we ever know where He is leading, that we've made the right choices much less be under His protection? Time with Jesus is never wasted. What He has for us is so much better than anything we can imagine, but most of the time, we never trust Him long enough to find out. We want a drive-thru Jesus, where we can pick up what we need from Him and go on with our lives. As much as everything else might work like that in our lives, Jesus doesn't. He is a relationship kind of guy and I mean long term. He is looking for friends He can do life with, not cyber time with. Those who choose to do life with God find He takes them on amazing adventures, way beyond their imagination.

> Now unto him that is able to do exceeding abun-
> dantly above all that we ask or think, according to
> the power that worketh in us (Ephesians 3:20 KJV).

One of those men just happened to be Dr. David Livingstone. David was born in Scotland, one of seven children in a tenement building belonging to cotton mill workers. He began working fourteen-hour shifts in the cotton mill at age 10 to help support his family. He worked there until the age of 26. While attending a village school he heard about medical missionaries going to China, so he saved his money to go to medical school and join the London Missionary Society. When it was time for him to go on the mission field, a war had broken out in China, and it was not safe. He then met a missionary who had been to South Africa and inspired him to go farther north into Africa where no missionary had ever been. As an adamant opponent of the slave trade, he thought he might be helpful in that area since abolitionists believed that the influence of Christianity would destroy it as a means of commerce. His first missionary journeys there met with no success. On his third trip, however, after two years of patient persuasion, he was finally able to convert the chief of a tribe. It was short-lived, however, as the chief reverted to his old ways after a few months. This seeming failure on Livingstone's part as a missionary caused him to rethink how he might best advance his cause to end the slave trade and lead others to Christ. He believed he had a spiritual calling for exploration to find routes on the interior of Africa and map them for missionaries to use to evangelize and use as commerce thereby displacing the slave trade routes. "Christianity, Commerce and Civilization" was his motto.

Livingstone was one of the first from the western world to travel the entire continent of Africa. "He discovered for Western Science numerous geographical features,"[43] including Victoria Falls, which he named for his queen. He filled in details of lakes and many rivers and "his observations enabled large regions to be mapped, which had previously been blank."[44] Preaching the Christian message along the way, but not forcing it on those who did not want to hear it, he was often well received and aided. Livingstone is known as Africa's greatest Christian missionary. He was known to only have the one convert in the chief of the tribe, Sechele, who for a while reverted back to old ways, but unbeknownst to Livingstone, came back to Christianity. Sechele then went on and "did more to propagate Christianity in nineteenth-century southern Africa than virtually any single European missionary."[45]

We never know how some turn in events or expectations will move us into our purpose. In the meantime, we are to be physically active in our pursuit of leading others to Christ through our words and actions. For with our hope fixed completely on Him, He will lead us on an adventure that we will not know the full fruit of until He is revealed to us face to face. Continue on, my friend, in the hope of that glorious grace.

DAY 27

*"You will live secure and full of hope;
God will protect you and give you rest."*
JOB 11:18 GNT

Whether it was a security blanket, pacifier, or favorite stuffed toy as a child, or a paid off mortgage, money in the bank or a relationship as an adult, we all have things we think make us secure. Job himself was the richest man in the east during his time, but he was also a great man of faith. Rarely do you see those two things together, but he was exceptional in every way and he had both God and Satan's attention. Satan was annoyed because the hedge of protection God had placed around Job because of his righteousness was so thick, he couldn't touch Job or anything he had. So Satan went to God and asked permission to take everything away from Job to see if Job would still serve God. God granted that permission and in one day Job lost everything he owned, including all of his children and servants. The value of just the livestock alone was:

Animal	Quantity	Price	Total
Camel	3000	$700 (each)	$2,100,000
Donkey	500	$895 (each)	$447,500
Oxen	500	$3000 (per team)	$1,500,000
Sheep	7000	$300 (each)	$2,100,000

Total for all Animals: $6,147,500

How is that for a one-day loss, not to mention the price-less cost of all of your children and servants? Most of us cannot imagine losing a child, but all of them and everything you own, unfathomable! But Job, being a righteous man said, "Naked I came from my mother's womb, and naked I will depart. The LORD gave and the LORD has taken away; may the name of the LORD be praised. In all this, Job did not sin by charging God with wrongdoing" (Job 1:21-22).

So Satan came again to God and asked permission to attack Job's flesh and bones. God granted permission, but not to take Job's life. So Job was afflicted with painful sores all over his body and still did not sin in what he said. Job had nothing in which to place his hope, but in God alone, and this he did without fail. At the end of this time of trial in Job's life, God restored to Job a double portion of all he had before because of his faithfulness to trust in the Lord alone to meet all of his needs.

When times of economic downturn come or devastating losses of family members or tragedies occur, many of us blame God. Some refuse to believe in a God who could seemingly be so cruel. Many have determined they have to provide for themselves and look to what they can accomplish on their own to be their security. In some ways becoming their own god, thinking they are controlling their own destiny. How foolish! Jesus says, "Yes, a person is a fool to store up earthly wealth but not have a rich relationship with God" (Luke 12:21 NLT).

And He said to His disciples, "For this reason I say to you, do not worry about your life, as to what you will eat; nor for your body, as to what you will put on. For life is more than food, and the body more than clothing. Consider the ravens, for they neither sow nor reap; they have no storeroom nor barn, and yet God feeds them; how much more valuable you are than the birds! And which of you by worrying can add a single hour to his life's span? If then you cannot do even a very little thing, why do you worry about other matters? Consider the lilies, how they grow: they neither toil nor spin; but I tell you, not even Solomon in all his glory clothed himself like one of these. But if God so clothes the grass in the field, which is alive today and tomorrow is thrown into the furnace, how much more will He clothe you? You men of little faith! And do not seek what you will eat and what you will drink, and do not keep worrying. For all these things the nations of the world eagerly seek; but your Father knows that you need these things. But seek His kingdom, and these things will be added to you. Do not be afraid, little flock, for your Father has chosen gladly to give you the kingdom. Sell your possessions and give to charity; make yourselves money belts which do not wear out, an unfailing treasure in heaven, where no thief comes near nor moth destroys. For where your treasure is, there your heart will be also" (Luke 12:22-34 NASB).

Treasures and fortunes have indeed come and gone from many who have toiled with the sweat of their brows to make sure they and their families had more than enough. Cornelius Vanderbilt amassed a fortune that should have taken care of his family for eons, and yet 48 years after his death, one of his grandchildren died penniless. All security is not in our wealth. To be secure in knowing who we are can bring about great peace, confidence, and rest from striving to measure up to some worldly standard. Jesus says seek His kingdom and everything we need will be provided for us. This doesn't mean to sit around waiting and not work, it simply means look to Him to provide the way. Seek Him in every decision and "he will guide you into all truth" (John 16:13).

Life can be difficult and we don't know what is coming at us next. But to know the one true God who feeds the birds and clothes the grass is concerned with such small matters is comforting indeed, how much more will He be concerned about our needs. He longs for us to know we can be secure, full of hope, and rest in the fact He has got us. No matter what turmoil you are going through, what loss, what tragedy, He knew it was coming before it even happened, so He has already prepared a way for you to get through it. Trust Him with your security, protection, and rest, for He is the only hope you can count on.

DAY 28

*"I wait for the LORD, my soul waits,
and in his word I hope."*
PSALM 130:5 ESV

We wait for the light to change, to buy groceries, to get our paycheck, for a new baby to arrive, and on and on. Waiting is a part of our everyday lives and yet I would have to say it is a virtue anyone has yet to master. Waiting should go with patience and yet all of us don't wait patiently. Some of us get more furious when we have to wait and for some it can ruin their whole day, like standing in line at the DMV or waiting on a repairman to fix something in your home. So waiting on God, who took 25 years before He brought to fruition something He promised to Abraham, well, we just don't feel we have that long to wait. Lifespans are shorter now than they were in Abraham's day, so hurry up God! We don't have that kind of time.

Waiting can be especially hard in desperate times when we need something from the Lord, an answer, provision or comfort. David knew this as he was often on the run from his enemies. In a time when the written word was not available to common man, I'm sure it was even more difficult not to have the comforting words of Scripture to speak peace and direction. Even though the Word is readily available today, many do not know it well enough or spend time in it to know the comfort and direction our precious Lord has for us. God can answer our prayers in so many different ways, yet His written Word can be a guide to confirm them as truth. In this day and age we can't even imagine what people went through to provide His Word to common man.

John Wycliffe (mid 1320-1384) and William Tyndale (1494-1536) are just two of the men who thought ordinary people should have access to the Scriptures. Before their translations of the Bible, the clergy read the Scriptures, still written in Latin, to the people for no one yet had a Bible for themselves. Many individuals in The Middle Ages were uneducated and Wycliffe, an Oxford professor, who had read the entire Bible, felt sorry people couldn't gain strength from something that could help them and give them comfort. He decided to translate the Bible for them from Latin into the language of the day for the common man. Because of what he did, he lost his professorship, was excommunicated from the church, and was considered a heretic. Thirty-one years after he died, the Pope requested his bones be dug up, burned, and his ashes thrown into the river.

Tyndale, an English scholar, was the first to translate the Bible into the English language from the original Hebrew and Greek translations. He was in direct violation of the Roman Catholic Church and the laws of England of which the penalty was death to be in possession of any scripture written in English. Tyndale wrote *The Practice of Prelates* and called King Henry VIII out on the annulment of his marriage so that he could marry Anne Boleyn, saying the king had failed to conform to Scripture. From that point on the King wanted Tyndale to pay. Tyndale went into hiding for a few years, continuing to write, but was eventually found, tried, and convicted of heresy, strangled, and burned at the stake. It was said that Tyndale's last words at the stake before dying were "Lord, open the King of England's eyes."[46] Four years later, English translations were published at Henry VIII's request.

Many Bibles were burned and people were killed who had possession of them. Copied by hand, many just had a page or two of the precious words of God now translated in a language they could understand, hidden like treasure. If they were found to have a copy of the Word, the penalty was death. And it was the church persecuting the people to rid the world of what they thought was so heretical to their own understanding. Not much different from Jesus's time, when they didn't recognize Him either.

Today we are not much better really. We still don't fully understand and still persecute others with our judgment and condemnation. Instead of waiting on God and what He has to say about a matter or letting Him take care of the outcome, we take matters into our own hands. We think we are waiting on Him, but how much is He really waiting on us? To come to know Him, love Him, and trust Him. Next time, you find yourself waiting on God, look to His Word and know that whatever you need is already there. He is the hope for which our soul waits, the answer to all our needs.

DAY 29

"but those that hope in the LORD will renew their strength. They will soar on wings like eagles; they will run and not grow weary, they will walk and not faint."
ISAIAH 40:31

Perspective. Life is all about perspective. Is the glass half empty or is it half full? What are we looking at and how are we looking at it. A little play on words, but so relevant. If we are looking at God and drawing upon His strength to endure, get through, get over, prepare, understand, enjoy, grow, and so on, we won't be as concerned about what is happening around us, because we know what is around us is just a shadow of spiritual things. We will quickly flounder, be overwhelmed and lose steam, however, if we try to work out things ourselves trying to fit them in a spiritual mold. Most people live life this way and quickly get caught up in the present and do life in their own strength. They believe God is for Sundays, holidays, deaths, miracles, and when we desperately need Him.

But God in His great compassion, understanding, and grace, knows how difficult it is to break through this physical dimension and see into the spiritual realm. He reminds the Israelites in this chapter of all He is and has done and what He can do. And then in this beautiful verse, He shows them a key to living in the Kingdom. He says it is their hope in Him that will renew their strength. That speaks about waiting and believing in what is to come. For the Old Testament believers, they were looking forward to the first coming of their messiah and for the New Testament believers, which is us, we are looking forward to His second coming. So our strength is renewed in waiting and looking forward to His coming. Then He says they will soar on wings like eagles. Eagles can soar for hours in the air at 65 mph, at 10,000-15,000 feet. They can spot their prey a mile down below and swoop down at 200 mph to scoop them up with their talons. Eagles are at the top of their food chain and have few natural predators, but their ability to fly keeps them out of their predator's paths.

There are several spiritual takeaways for us here. Soaring takes us up into heavenly realms being undergirded by the Holy Spirit's wind. We can enjoy our time with Him for hours there, be refreshed and renewed in the Spirit. From that vantage point, if there is anything we need to take care of on the earth, we can quickly get to it, because we will be filled with the Lord's strength. And our ability to soar, means we stay out of the path of our enemy. So how do we soar? By praise, worship, and sitting in His presence.

You will know it when you get there, because there will be peace, joy, love, and contentment unlike anything else you've ever known.

Now until we get to that level, the Lord will still give us the strength from being in His Presence to run the course He has set before us. Like He did in a great God showdown between Elijah and the prophets of Baal. God revealed He was God by being the only god to be able to bring rain on the dry land. Elijah then tells King Ahab he better hitch up his chariot and horse before the rain stops him from being able to travel due to the mud.

> Meanwhile, the sky grew black with clouds, the wind rose, a heavy rain started falling and Ahab rode off to Jezreel. The power of the LORD came on Elijah and, tucking his cloak into his belt, he ran ahead of Ahab all the way to Jezreel (I Kings 18:45-46).

Elijah, with the strength of the Lord, was able to outrun a horse and chariot. And that is not the only time people in the Bible ran in the Lord's strength. I'm telling you we serve a God of power and He wants you to receive that same power by being in His presence. When you are doing great things for God and proclaiming Him as Lord, He shows up and things happen. Elijah's faith, his hope, was so strong in His God, he knew God would reveal Himself. Faith moves mountains and faith moves God. Putting our hope in God's strength allows us to do greater things than we could ever accomplish on our own.

Finally, the Lord tells us to walk and not faint. For those who are not at the belief level of running or soaring, the Lord will walk with you and give you strength so that you do not faint. To me the worst thing about being on this level is that you are closer to the enemy so you are more vulnerable to attack. It's also harder to separate what is heavenly from what is deceptive at times, because you are young in your walk and have not matured yet to the deeper things of God. You still don't know Him well enough, as to be sure of what you believe. You want to, but you don't wait. You show no patience for sitting at His feet like Mary. You either settle for this place with Him, move up or walk away altogether.

> Now as they were traveling along, He entered a village; and a woman named Martha welcomed Him into her home. She had a sister called Mary, who was seated at the Lord's feet, listening to His word. But Martha was distracted with all her preparations; and she came up to *Him* and said, "Lord, do You not care that my sister has left me to do all the serving alone? Then tell her to help me." But the Lord answered and said to her, "Martha, Martha, you are worried and bothered about so many things; but *only* one thing is necessary, for Mary has chosen the good part, which shall not be taken away from her (Luke 10:38-42 NASB).

Only one thing is necessary. Sitting at His feet, listening. Oh, there is plenty of Kingdom work to do, but that is not what the Lord is after. He could accomplish all of that without you. He would rather just enjoy your presence. The two of you just spending time together. This is His most favorite thing. You see there are already lots of people out there working for the Kingdom, they may not get it all done or have the right heart, but He is not worried about that. He knows His children and it is the Holy Spirit who convicts and saves, not us. We just get to work along with Him. So rather than trying to work to please Him or impress others, or feel good about yourself, wouldn't it be better to draw near to Him and find out what exactly is on His heart?

In one of my quiet times with Him, I felt Him telling me He wanted to show me what the town I lived in looked like from His perspective. Because I don't live in a big city, I had never seen my town from the air. Some intense spiritual warfare had been taking place in our community. Two sisters in Christ, Leah and Leslie and I had already had a prayer powwow on the ground, telling the enemy that God was in charge and He gave us authority over all "…evil rulers and authorities of the unseen world, against mighty powers in this dark world, and against evil spirits in the heavenly places" (Ephesians 6:12 NLT).

I felt from the Lord to call Sandy, a friend of mine who had a small private plane. I asked her if she would take my two sisters in Christ and I up in her plane to circle our town to pray over the people and everything the Lord would show us. Sandy is a believer too, so she was more than happy to do it. We went within a couple of days and flew at about 1000 feet above the ground. From that position, we all felt peace and calm. You could feel someone greater was in charge. We circled our town several times and felt impressed by the Lord to pray many things. It was as if He Himself had given us that as our job for Him that day. It was serious and exciting all at the same time. Prayer is a weapon and being able to use it from a different position was both challenging and thrilling. It made me want to learn how to fly so I could do it all the time. It was like the Lord was showing me what it looked like to soar.

Looking back on that now, I believe the Lord was saying "Come on up a little higher." I accept the challenge and pray you do to. We must hope in the Lord and He will renew our strength. We shall soar like the eagles, run like the wind, and walk in boldness.

DAY 30

"So now faith, hope, and love abide, these three;
but the greatest of these is love."
1 CORINTHIANS 13:13 ESV

For years I did not understand this verse. The words seemed noble, but exactly what did they mean. This verse, of course, comes from the famous love chapter in the Bible telling us what love is and what it is not. We use this verse often in weddings and it has been used in song. But why are faith, hope, and love grouped together and why is love the greatest? Paul says in 1 Corinthians 12:31, "And yet I will show you the most excellent way." He then goes on to say no matter what we do if we do it without love, it is meaningless. When we put aside everything we do and everything we are, these three things should remain in us, the greatest being love.

As a doer, this verse scared me. I wondered if in all the things I had done for the Lord, would love remain in any of them. Were those things done in the name of the Lord because of love or because I hoped they would earn me something? Rarely are we truly not thinking or doing something without wanting to feel good or get something in return. What if I supposedly did these acts of kindness, not in real love, but some type of self-love, ensuring what I thought would be my place in heaven. God help! Was I just living off of faith and hope?

Faith and hope seemed easy for me. I had this child-like mentality, that I call my Disney World® mentality, where anything is possible if you believe. I wanted to go to heaven, because the thought of going to hell sounded scary. So I totally bought the whole package the church was selling and went forward to accept Jesus into my heart. Of course, I didn't truly know what that meant, but was more than willing to find out if that was what it took to stay out of the burning fire. So I went to church, tried to follow all the Christian rules, and read my Bible. I was seeking to be a better Christian, but didn't really have a relationship with the Father. I thought I had one, mind you, until someone pointed out I didn't know Him at all.

Right before I met this person God sent to help me, I had gotten to a place where I was tired and bored. I was following all the "Christian rules" for a good life, but I didn't always see God's goodness right away. Life was short and I was not happy. I wanted something more, deeper, and full of unconditional love, that wasn't based on what I did or didn't do. If a life of rules was the way of Jesus, which I thought it was, I wanted out. He could take back His salvation, I was going to try it my way and see if I could find something or someone to fill that void in my heart. My faith and hope in Him was gone. I didn't really believe He was all I needed because I had tried Him for years and His way wasn't working for me. If He really loved me, He would forgive me like He seemed to be doing for all of those other people who were out there living it up.

You see what I really believe Paul is saying in our verse today, reminds me of another verse in the Bible. "Though one may be overpowered, two can defend themselves. A cord of three strands is not quickly broken" (Ecclesiastes 4:12).

Three is used over and over in the Bible as a sign of completeness. Even though this verse speaks of people, when one is down the other two will help him up, it is also a visual to us of the divine threefold cord of faith, hope, and love. Wherever we are weak in faith or hope or love, then the Lord says in 2 Corinthians 12:9, "...My grace is sufficient for you, for my power is made perfect in weakness." You see the Lord knows our weaknesses, He knows His children. He knew us before He placed us in our mother's wombs (Jeremiah 1:5). He already knew everything about us even where and when we would need Him the most. Whether it is in the area of faith (Revelation 19:11), hope (1 Timothy 1:1), or love (1 John 4:8) for He is the summation of all three. He would pursue us and woo us with His love until in our crisis of belief we recognized Him as truly our Savior and we would cry out to Him to save us. For you see it is not our faith, hope, and love, but His that He gives to us and perfects in us through Jesus Christ. And of course, the greatest of these is His love, for that is what fills the void in our hearts that longs to experience His unconditional love and opens our hearts to everything else He has for us.

After a year of not living unto the Lord, I felt like I was drowning in sorrow. I had allowed the enemy so much access to my life and had found he was a demanding dictator, liar, and manipulator. The Lord seemed to be everywhere I turned and it was remarkable how He was trying to reach me, but I had already tried it His way and just didn't see how He had anything to really offer. I couldn't seem to find true unconditional love and decided I could not live like this any longer. I knew inside I was physically dying. I literally was starving myself to death and contemplated suicide many times.

A Christian band I had liked as a teenager and always wanted to see was coming to town. I had not sung to the Lord for a year, but had this desire to go and see them. At the concert they began to sing a song called "Open the Eyes of My Heart." For some reason, I began to sing that song. My spirit was crying out to win in this spiritual battle for my soul. I went home and went to bed with that song still in my head. That night I had a dream where I had jumped in a lake and was taking in water so I could drown. I kept hearing the Lord say to me just cry out "help" and I can save you. Finally on my last breath, I cried out "help" and I shot up out of the water. I was lying on a dock and my husband was trying to give me mouth-to-mouth resuscitation. Jesus was there and told my husband this was something only He could do. Jesus then picked me up and carried me. The next thing I knew,

I was lying in an all white place and Jesus was there waiting for me to wake up. He gently opened my chest and took out my heart. It was black. He then put a new heart in and said it was a heart like His.

A couple of verses that confirm this are:

> The LORD is close to the brokenhearted and saves those who are crushed in spirit (Psalm 34:18).

> Then I will sprinkle clean water on you, and you will be clean; I will cleanse you from all your filthiness and from all your idols. Moreover, I will give you a new heart and put a new spirit within you; and I will remove the heart of stone from your flesh and give you a heart of flesh. I will put My Spirit within you and cause you to walk in My statutes, and you will be careful to observe My ordinances (Ezekiel 36:25-27 NASB).

After that night, I have never been the same. I recognized that God truly was Lord and He loved me unconditionally. Because of His great love, He gave me a new heart like His and freedom through His Spirit in me to carefully follow what He has for me because it is for my good, my protection, and for others. He is ever increasing my faith, hope, and love in Him as our relationship grows. I understand now why faith, hope and love abide because they are the essence of who He is and the essence of who we are in Him. And as Paul said, this is "the most excellent way."

Endnote

M aybe after reading this, you find that you really don't
know the Hope sent to be with you forever, which
is Jesus Christ. Jesus says, "Behold I stand at the door (of
your heart) and knock. If anyone hears My voice and opens
the door, I will come in…" (Revelation 3:20 NKJV). "If
you confess with your mouth the Lord Jesus and believe in
your heart that God has raised Him from the dead, you will
be saved" (Romans 10:9 NKJV). He is just waiting for you
to cry "help".. His love for you is greater than anything you
can imagine and He longs to lavish it upon you and carry
you in His arms when you need Him. He is your hope. If
you don't know Him personally as your Savior, call upon
Him now with this prayer:

> Father God, I long to know You, your son Jesus
> Christ and the Holy Spirit. I confess that I am a
> sinner and have not known You or Your ways. I
> ask that You forgive me of my sins and cover me
> with the blood of Jesus. I believe Jesus Christ
> died on the cross that I might be saved from my
> sins. Exchanging His life for mine, that I might

be able to spend eternity with You. On the third day, Jesus rose from the dead and ascended to the Father, leaving the Holy Spirit to live in me once I confess You as Lord of my life. Holy Spirit, You are my comforter and will lead me into all truth. Father, take my life that I might be changed into the image of your Son, Jesus, who paid it all for me. I now know Jesus, You are the way, the truth and the life and no one comes to the Father except through You. Thank You that I am now a child of God!

If you prayed this prayer, you are now born again! Trust God to lead you, seek Him with all of your heart and He will be found by you. And this is just the beginning…

If you prayed this prayer, or have further questions, we would love to hear from you. Please contact us at:

ElizabethAnnWallace.com

Acknowledgements

I would like to acknowledge and offer my most heartfelt gratitude to the following people who were such a part of the journey to the publication of this devotional:

To Rujon and Steve Morrison, you know of all people, the pit God had to pull me out of in my journey of really knowing Him. Both of you fought for me and sacrificed yourselves to reach down and help me out of the pit, I dug for myself. To both of you I am eternally grateful and I tell everyone I know about your wonderful, God changing retreats.

To Charles "Doc" Boswell, you believed in me and saw what God was doing way before I even had a clue. Your encouragement and confidence allowed me to grow and step out into previously uncharted God territory.

To Jean Hungerpiller, when I was looking for a Bible study, you took me in and the next thing I know, you made me the teacher. Your heart for the Lord and for others to know Him, has brought so many into the kingdom and their destinies.

Jackie Landrette, Leslie Williamson, Kathy Wells, Michelle Burton, Kay Widener, Beth Shealy, Leah and Megan Wilson, Cheryl Braswell, Meredith Allen, Heather Perry, Roger Roden, Rose Naser, Kurt Kjellstrom, Debbie Beck, Mark Casey, Edie Melson, Cindy Sproles, Carolyn Knefely, my prayer warriors, Bible study brothers and sisters, friends and saints, we have walked many steps together on the kingdom road. Y'all have encouraged me and helped me more than you will ever know and this book is a result of all of your efforts.

To Linda Gilden, my editor, Terry Whalin, Aubrey Kosa, Bonnie Rauch, David Hancock, Jim Howard, Chris Treccani, Christopher Kirk and the great team at Morgan James Publishing. Thank you for all your help. Truly this was a team effort.

To my parents, Alfred and Charlotte Florence, this book is a part of your legacy in the kingdom, for without you I would not be here to write it. ☺ Your prayers and love for me have been pivotal in its release.

To my two daughters, Madison and Meredith Wallace, mighty warriors in God's kingdom, my life has been so full because of you. Only God knew, how much I would need you in getting this book ready for release. Lol I just pray this book now launches you into greater works for His kingdom!

To my loving husband, Thomas, without your support and confidence, this book would cease to exist. You truly have been a sentry guard in the kingdom, mighty and loyal warrior for the things of God. I am beyond blessed that you stand by my side.

And finally to those who have gone on to heaven whose prayers, support and input into my life played a pivotal role in the release of this work, my grandmother, Carol Teasley Florence, friends, Deb Newsome and John Kunst.

About the Author

Elizabeth Ann Wallace, wife, mother, author, speaker, photographer, and Bible study teacher, currently resides in South Carolina. She has been a staff writer and photographer for Cool Springs Living magazine in Nashville, Tennessee, as well as a contributor to ChristianDevotions.US. God has now gifted her with Grace Anointed Ministries to touch others with His grace beyond the boundaries of where she lives. She loves to travel and has worked for an international ministry, been a Women's ministry director, spoken and served in ministry both domestically as well as abroad, and served in various other positions in different ministries throughout her lifetime. She is a graduate of both Class and Christian Communicators speaking services. Passionate about Christ, her prayer is to get the word out about how amazing God is and all that He has for you. Connect with her at ElizabethAnnWallace.com

References

1. Dickinson, Emily. "'Hope" is the thing with feathers." *marnecarmean.com*, Marne Carmean, 1861, www.marnecarmean.com/page04.html.

2. Lewis, C.S. *The Case for Christianity*. B & H Pub Group, 2000, pp. 32.

3. Lewis, C.S. *Surprised by Joy*. Harvest Books, 1955, pp. 229.

4. Ibid. pp. 228-229.

5. Conn, Marie A. *C.S. Lewis and Human Suffering: Light Among the Shadows*. New Jersey, Hidden Spring, 2008, pp. 33.

6. Merriam Webster. "Blessed." *Merriam Webster*, Merriam Webster Incorporated, www.merriam-webster.com/dictionary/blessed.

7. Müller, George. *A Narrative of Some of the Lord's Dealings with George Müller*. 6th ed., e-book, London, J. Davy and Sons, 1860, pp. 455.

8. Steer, Roger (1997). *George Müller: Delighted in God*. Tain, Rosshire: Christian Focus, pp. 131.

9. Tenney, Tommy. *Trust and Tragedy: Encountering God in Times of Crisis.* Nashville, Thomas Nelson, 2001, pp. 46.

10. Ibid. pp. 47.

11. Praimnath, Stanley. "STANLEY PRAIMNATH - Worked in World Trade Ctr Twr 2 on 9/11." *Ambassador: Representing Today's Leading Christian Speakers*, Ambassador Agency, Inc., www.ambassadorspeakers.com/ACP/speakers.aspx?name=STANLEY%20PRAIMNATH&speaker=375.

12. Keller, Timothy. "Christianity among the Cultures." *Walking with God through Pain and Suffering*, New York, Penguin Group, 2013, pp. 31.

13. Wells, Amos R. "Ring the Bells." *A Cyclopedia of Twentieth Century Illustrations*, Fleming H. Revell Company, 1918, pp. 139.

14. Atwood, Kathryn J. *Women Heroes of World War II.* Chicago, Chicago Review Press, 2011, pp. 121-122.

15. Boom, Corrie Ten, et al. *The Hiding Place.* Peabody, Massachusetts, Hendrickson Publishers, 2009, pp. 240.

16. Merton, Thomas. *Thoughts in Solitude.* New York, Farrar, Straus and Cudahy, 1999, pp. 79.

17. Freeman, Elisabeth. "Jordan Bilyeu, Tsunami Survivor: Jordan wasn't sure if he'd live or die." *Ignite Your Faith*, Christianity Today: Global Media Ministry, www.christianitytoday.com/iyf/truelifestories/ithappenedtome/20.21.html.

18. Stroud, James Edward. *The Knights Templar & the Protestant Reformation: And the Case for the Modern Day Monk*. Xulon Press, 2011, pp. 264.

19. Beamer, Lisa, and Ken Abraham. *Let's Roll!: Ordinary People, Extraordinary Courage*. Colorado Springs, Alive Communications, 2002, pp. 212.

20. Helms, Harold E. *God's Final Answer*. Xulon Press, 2004, pp. 78.

21. Homan, Vincent D. *A Foot in Two Worlds: A Pastor's Journey From Grief to Hope*. WestBow Press, 2013, pp. 112.

22. "Star Trek-like invisible shield found thousands of miles above Earth." *University of Colorado Boulder*, Regents of the University if Colorado, 26 Nov. 2014, www.colorado.edu/today/2014/11/26/star-trek-invisible-shield-found-thousands-miles-above-earth.

23. Major in the U.S. Army for OS91. "Testimony of the Lord's Protection of a U.S. Army Major." *In Pursuit Ministries CA*, www.inpursuitca.com/testimony-of-the-lords-protection-of-a-u-s-army-major-while-deployed-in-afghanistan/.

24. Say, Paul. "THE REAL SOLDIERS DEPICTED IN THE NEW FILM '13 HOURS' WERE DRIVEN BY ONE THING: FAITH." *Six Seeds*, Patheos, 11 July 2016, www.sixseeds.patheos.com/watchinggod/2016/01/the-real-soldiers-depicted-in-the-new-film-13-hours-were-driven-by-one-thing-faith/.

25. Chambers, Oswald. "Psalm 128." *The Complete Works of Oswald Chamber*, Grand Rapids, Discovery House Publishers, 2000, pp. 537.

26. "Denzel Washington." AZQuotes.com. Wind and Fly LTD, 2017. 12 December 2017. http://www.azquotes.com/quote/1293304

27. Tozer, A.W. *The Knowledge of the Holy*. San Francisco, HarperCollins Publisher, 1961, pp. 104-105.

28. Emerson, Ralph Waldo. "Worship." *Prose Works: Representative Men. English Traits. Conduct of Life*, e-book, vol. 2, Boston, James R Osgood and Company, 1872, pp. 438. 2 vols.

29. Mauro, James. "Bright Lights, Big Mystery." *Psychology Today*, HealthProfs.com, 1 July 1992, www.psychologytoday.com/articles/199207/bright-lights-big-mystery.

30. Mother Teresa of Calcutta. "Joy." *A Gift for God: Prayers and Meditations*, HarperSanFrancisco, 1996, pp. 77-78.

31. Edwards, Jonathan. "God the Portion of the Christian." *The Works of President Edwards*, vol. 6, New York, S. Converse, 1829, pp. 289. 10 vols.

32. DoSomething.org. "11 Facts About Global Poverty." *DoSomething.org*, www.dosomething.org/us/facts/11-facts-about-global-poverty.

33. "MEET THE TEAM: JON'S TESTIMONIAL." *J10:10*, 3 Feb. 2012, www.j1010.org/?p=308#comment-52903.

34. Ibid.

35. Hawn, C. Michael. "History of Hymns: 'Great is Thy Faithfulness.'" *Discipleship Ministries: The United Methodist Church*, Hope Publishing Company, 1951, www.umcdiscipleship.org/resources/history-of-hymns-great-is-thy-faithfulness.

36. "GREAT IS THY FAITHFULNESS" - THE STORY BEHIND THE HYMN." *Gaither*, Gaither Music, www.gaither.com/news/"great-thy-faithfulness"-story-behind-hymn.

37. Schram, Jamie, et al. 'Jealous butcher 'killed mom, 4 kids because they had too much.'" *New York Post*, News Corp, 27 Oct. 2013, www.nypost.com/2013/10/27/jealous-butcher-killed-mom-4-kids-because-they-had-too-much/.

38. Keller, W. Phillip. "He Taketh Me to Lie Down in Green Pastures." *A Shepherd Looks at Psalm 23*, Anniversary ed., Grand Rapids, Zondervan Publishing House, 1970, pp. 35-47.

39. Basquez, Anna Maria. "Colorado scientist's research finds spot for parting of the Red Sea." *Catholic News Service*, U.S. Conference of Catholic Bishops, 11 Jan. 2011, www.catholicnews.com/services/english-news/2011/colorado-scientist-s-research-finds-spot-for-parting-of-the-red-sea.cfm.

40. Pernoud, Regine. "Vocation and Departure." *Joan of Arc: By Herself and Her Witnesses*, translated by Edward Hyams, Scarborough House, 1994, pp. 35.

41. Richey, Stephen W. "Joan of Arc - A Military Appreciation." *Joan of Arc - A Military Appreciation*, The Saint Joan of Arc Center, www.stjoan-center.com/military/stephenr.html.

42. Williamson, Allen. "Segment 3: Vaucouleurs." *Joan of Arc*, Allen Williamson, www.joan-of-arc.org/joanofarc_life_summary_vaucouleurs.html.

43. Johnson, George D. "Geographical Discoveries." *What Will A Man Give In Exchange For His Soul?*, Xlibris Corporation, 2011, p. 78.

44. Ibid.

45. Parsons, Neil. "A Trinity of Dusky Kings." *King Khama, Emperor Joe, and the Great White Queen: Victorian Britain Through African Eyes*, Chicago, The University of Chicago Press, 1998, p. 40.

46. Jenson, Peter. "Lord, open the King of England's eyes!" *GAFCON*, 28 Mar. 2017, www.gafcon.org/blog/lord-open-the-king-of-englands-eyes.

MorganJames
Speakers Group

We connect Morgan James published authors with live and online events and audiences who will benefit from their expertise.

Morgan James makes all of our titles available
through the Library for All Charity Organization.

www.LibraryForAll.org